The
Case for
Nature

The Case for Nature

Pioneering Solutions
for the <u>Other</u>
Planetary Crisis

SIDDARTH SHRIKANTH

125 YEARS

DUCKWORTH

This edition first published in the
United Kingdom by Duckworth in 2023

Duckworth, an imprint of Duckworth Books Ltd
1 Golden Court, Richmond, TW9 1EU, United Kingdom
www.duckworthbooks.co.uk

For bulk and special sales please contact
info@duckworthbooks.com

A catalogue record for this book is available from the British Library

Text design and typesetting by Danny Lyle

Printed and bound in Great Britain by Clays

Hardback ISBN: 9780715654729
e-ISBN: 9780715654736

To those who came before me – my father, Shrikanth, his mother, Savitri, and her father, Thirumurthi. Their undying love for nature lives on in me.

Contents

Why Nature? Why Now?

To our right, just across the monsoonal river, lay a forest of sal trees, the constant hum of the cicadas in the undergrowth punctuated only by the escalating call of an Indian cuckoo. Just minutes away from where we now stood, we had sighted the area's newly dominant male tiger, Neela Nala, marking his territory as he strutted across a clearing, chital deer scattering in his wake.

On the near side of the river was a different landscape altogether: field after field of paddy, dotted with the colourful mud-and-terracotta houses typical of the Gond and Baiga tribal communities. By contrast, the tractors and shiny motorcycles parked around the place represented the recent, if still modest, prosperity of much of rural India.

A few decades ago, the two vistas might have been indistinguishable. In 2022, the difference was night and day. The 'core' zone of the celebrated Kanha national park, across the river, had remained largely pristine, supporting a rebound in tiger populations as poaching pressures within the park eased.

The challenge lay in the so-called 'buffer' zone to our left. The legacy of relocations of tribal villages out of the park, combined with India's recent economic growth, had seen rice paddies and roads displace what had once been a thickly forested corridor to tiger reserves further afield. A previously vast, interconnected natural ecosystem across the Central Indian Highlands was becoming little more than a set of scattered wildlife refuges in a landscape increasingly defined by human influence.

A week later, I encountered a similar scene in central Indonesia. Emerging from the ocean after a series of exhilarating drift-dives among manta rays and sharks in Komodo

Kanha National Park, now set within in an increasingly agricultural landscape. © Aaran Patel, by permission.

National Park, I came across the sorry sight of a five-foot-long dragon stepping gingerly over the bottle caps and plastic bags that washed up daily on the shores of Komodo island. Seen from above, the verdant, protected islands of the Sape Strait make a striking contrast with the boomtown of Labuan Bajo, where concrete radiates out from what had just years ago been the richly forested western tip of Flores.

Both Kanha and Komodo – success stories of an early wave of twentieth-century environmentalism – are exemplars of fortress-style conservation, a philosophy that seeks to define protected areas, protect them actively, and typically rid them of human influence. But both are now bumping up against the limits of what fortress conservation can achieve, surrounded as they are by growing economic pressures. Built infrastructure, agriculture, timber harvesting and pollution of all sorts are chipping away at their broader ecosystems, even as the core sites remain well protected. Against the backdrop of an escalating climate crisis, they risk being overlooked amid a well-intentioned global shift in focus to tackling greenhouse gas emissions. But the biodiversity crisis we are plunging into is just as perilous and urgent – for everyone on the planet. India and Indonesia are not alone in their struggle to balance economic development and conservation, to find ways to make space for nature while doing right by their people.

It was with places such as these in mind, with their complex local dynamics and competing priorities, that I set

A Komodo dragon wades through the plastic that washes up daily on the shores of the island.

out to write this book and make the case for nature: a case that appeals to both the head and the heart, and that offers a radical, hopeful and pragmatic path forward to regenerate our planet and revive our economies and societies along the way.

Central to the case I want to make are a set of ideas and recent developments that are grounded in the notion of 'natural capital'. The baseline of this approach is that, in and of itself, the natural world is *priceless* – but that doesn't mean it doesn't also have *value*. We are all familiar with the concepts of financial capital, human capital and social capital. Natural capital is simply a framework that can allow us to recognise a sliver of the value that we derive from the natural world: the ways in which our natural *assets*, like forests and oceans, can provide a range of *ecosystem services* that represent economic and social goods. These services range from tangible ones like clean air and water, carbon storage, fertile soils and pollination, to the intangible cultural and spiritual value that complements them. If we are to meet the imperative to protect and restore our planet, we can no longer treat nature as a distant wonder to be enjoyed on occasion before we retreat once again to modernity: natural capital fundamentally underpins our wellbeing and deserves a central place in our economic framework.

In an economy roiled by crisis after crisis, it can feel at times like the only option we have is to rip up our current system and start over again, embracing degrowth or dramatically curtailing the market economy. But the 'market' is a social construct, and one that has largely been governed with a narrow set of financial aims in mind. With time running out, I argue that we need to make a serious effort to fold nature's value into the system we already have: one that has, to its credit, brought remarkable progress and improved living standards for many, but has clearly gone too far in the direction of environmental destruction.

If net-zero carbon emissions is what we're aiming for in the climate fight, this book lays out some ways in which we can also shift to a 'nature-positive' economy: one that reverses biodiversity loss globally and begins restoring ecosystems and the communities that steward them. There is nothing incremental about this vision. We made this economy; now we can remake it.

We can begin simply by viewing nature differently. I hope the ideas in this book will lead you, like me, to believe that protecting and restoring nature is firmly in our economic interests, but also the right thing to do on moral and spiritual grounds; that nature needs to be bound closely to our societies, taking a cue from a range of indigenous worldviews, rather than set apart in fortresses.

While this book is focused on what and how we can gain, not on what we have already lost, the basic facts of ecosystem collapse are undeniable. From the global exchange of species carried on our ships to the 375 billion tonnes of carbon dioxide we have pumped into the atmosphere, we have bent the planet to our will and irrevocably changed it in the process. On land and in the sea, biodiversity is crashing as we continue to expand, extract, export and emit. We have driven the loss of a third of global forests and, with them, an ark's worth of species. From the dodo to the Formosan clouded leopard, much of the world's displaced flora and fauna can now be found only in cabinets of curiosities. And this is to say nothing of the many species which remain on the grim parade towards extinction, from orangutans and black rhinos to the Asiatic lion and the Yangtze River dolphin. Our natural world is tamer than it has ever been: 96 per cent of mammal biomass on our planet is now accounted for by us and our livestock, a number that barely rose above 2 per cent for the first 5,000 or so years of human civilisation. Industrial fishing has enabled us to pillage the seas, causing unprecedented reductions to once-populous species; nearly 90 per cent of global fish stocks are overexploited or depleted. Even in the benthos, the deepest seas about which we know less than we do about the moon, the effects of humanity can be felt as trawler nets drag across the sea floors. Though we have understood the dangers for a long time, agricultural runoff, industrial waste and oil spills continue to pour into our seas and waterways, causing mass die-offs and the accumulation of toxic compounds. Plastic pollution, too, finds its way into the oceans and a gyre of plastic waste three times the size of France now churns in the Pacific, entangling and poisoning sea life. Never before has Earth's biosphere been so disproportionately impacted by a single species.

All of this has taken place against the backdrop of a rapidly changing and warming climate. The year 2020 was the hottest in recorded history, with global temperatures as much as 1.3°C above pre-industrial levels.[1] In just the last couple of years, unprecedented wildfires have burned vast areas of California, Australia, Indonesia, Europe and even Siberia; powerful storms have wreaked havoc in the Caribbean and the Indo-Pacific alike. Pakistan has suffered the worst flooding in its history even as drought has taken hold in China and famine has stalked the horn of Africa. None of this should be news to even the most casual follower of world events, but few put it as starkly as David Wallace-Wells in his book *The Uninhabitable Earth*.

Countering the notion that we've entered a 'new normal', he writes, 'the truth is actually much scarier [...] That is, the end of normal, never normal again. We have already exited the state of environmental conditions that allowed the human animal to evolve in the first place [...] the climate system that raised us, and raised everything we know as human culture and civilisation, is now, like a parent, dead.'[2] It is hard to fault Wallace-Wells for being doom-and-gloom. His basic point is spot on; it is, indeed, what climate models suggest about where we find ourselves today.

'This is the warmest summer of your life, and the coldest summer of the rest of your life,' declares one widely shared meme. Dark humour might be a fair last resort in times like these, but I believe there are reasons to be cautiously optimistic, even if the odds remain long. On climate change, the years since the Paris Climate Accords in 2015 have been marked by a series of important tonal and tangible shifts in the way governments and businesses are approaching the carbon challenge. Dozens of governments have committed to achieving net-zero emissions by 2050 or thereabouts – a commitment that includes deep cuts to emissions (turning off the tap), and the scaling up of natural and engineered carbon removal (the draining of the atmospheric bathtub). Current policies put us on track for around 2.7 degrees of warming above pre-industrial levels by the end of the century – still catastrophic, but far lower than the 4 degrees that looked all but certain before Paris.[3] That alone is grounds for hope, as Wallace-Wells himself points out: a four- or six-degree-heated world would be unimaginably worse than a two-and-something-degree heated world in terms of the sheer extent of societal collapse that it would bring about.

To be sure, we need to work ever-harder to limit warming to 1.5 or 2 degrees, and we seem to take backward steps all the time, from the energy-market fallout of the Ukraine invasion to the election of climate deniers and free-market fundamentalists to high office. But, at the very least, our steps forward on carbon cutting are belatedly gathering pace.

The same cannot, unfortunately, be said of the biodiversity crisis. For all the attention that the annual climate conference of parties (COP) meetings, such as the ones in Paris in 2015 or Glasgow in 2021, receive, few people realise that a parallel set of biodiversity COPs has been limping along for decades. The last meeting, due to be held in Kunming in China in 2020, was postponed twice; it felt like hardly anyone noticed. Behind these divergent fates lies a shared origin story: both the UN Framework Convention on Climate Change and the Convention on Biological Diversity were conceived at the Rio Earth Summit in 1992, billed back then as the conference to save the world.

Three decades on, there is still the need for greater recognition that the biodiversity and climate crises are deeply intertwined. Tackling climate change simply cannot be done without tackling the agriculture and deforestation that currently account for a fifth of global emissions, and restoring the natural sinks (forests, wetlands, peatlands and the like) that can reverse warming by drawing down billions of tonnes of carbon. Climate change, in turn, is speeding up the collapse of the Earth's biodiversity as species everywhere struggle to adapt.

But the decarbonisation agenda has pulled steadily ahead of the biodiversity agenda in the years since Rio as businesses and governments have slowly but surely begun setting net-zero targets, investing in renewables and taking bold bets on new climate-related technologies. I take heart from the scores of peers now pivoting into careers focused on tackling the climate crisis. Christiana Figueres, the former Executive Secretary of the UN Framework Convention on Climate Change and arguably the world's foremost climate negotiator who led years of diplomacy that culminated in the 2015 Paris Climate Accords, acknowledged in an interview with me that she had seen a dramatic rise in climate-related careers in her two-plus decades working on the challenge. 'I used to know everybody who was working on climate, I definitely don't anymore,' she told me. 'And that's a wonderful thing […] with each new generation that comes in you get new skills, new viewpoints, new capacity to engage with such a complex issue. I'm delighted that there are so many new people in climate – and especially so many young people.'

But I chose to focus this book on *nature* in part because I noticed that those around me – the current or soon-to-be leaders in their respective fields of business, technology or policy – were finally waking up to the energy-climate challenge while often remaining in the dark about the extent and importance of the biodiversity crisis. This was never for a lack of interest; if climate change is now the stuff of careers, nature remains the realm of our truest passions. When I talked of my own love for nature, my peers and colleagues would reliably light up. 'I love nature too… I had an amazing time in [insert choice of national park, forest or dive site]' I'd hear, over and over again. We'd exchange notes about dives and hikes; we'd speak of the peace that a walk through a green space always brings.

This is, in my mind, the largely positive legacy of the nature conservation movement, which has inspired successive generations to look upon nature with wonderment and benevolence. This movement, exemplified by the creation of national parks like Kanha and Komodo across the world throughout the 1900s (though often to the violent exclusion of indigenous peoples – a theme we will return to) and the successful protection of a handful of charismatic species, has indeed achieved remarkable tactical gains. Human beings' irrepressible love for the natural world has been channelled into a powerful and primarily ethical argument for preservation. The logic, to put it in deliberately reductive terms, is clear and superficially compelling: we should set aside areas for plants and animals to thrive, and for us to visit and marvel at, even as we continue hurtling towards modernity in our own economies and societies.

No wonder, then, that in many of these conversations nature was spoken of as separate from the modern, typically urban, life of *Homo economicus*. When I broached the idea that it might also make hard-nosed, practical sense to value and invest in nature, I'd usually get puzzled looks from the same people who had, by now, made the link between an escalating climate crisis and its direct and all-too-real threats to our economies and societies. People who had become firmly convinced that climate action was in our economic, perhaps even selfish, interests. It was arguments like these that had led to a cascade of new net-zero commitments, and the accompanying billions in investments, in the years since Rio and Paris.

In each of those conversations, I learnt something of our collective failure to communicate the urgency of this 'other' crisis, to pluck nature from the realm of the nice-to-haves and place it firmly within the universe of existential questions. To build on the work of the first wave of environmental concern, it has become increasingly clear to me that we have to make a broader and deeper case for nature; to elevate *natural* capital, alongside its similarly overlooked cousin, *human* capital, to equal prominence with the financial capital we know all too well.

'With energy, we have compelling business models that have been developed over several years [...] There is market logic to it now, with a profitable business model,' Figueres explained. 'The problem with nature-based solutions, as opposed to energy-based solutions, is that there is no business model because we have not yet agreed on a valuation for walking carbon or flying carbon or swimming carbon or growing carbon.'

This success we have had in framing the climate challenge in economic terms is ultimately why this is not a book on the energy–climate challenge. Even as I explore the many links between the climate crisis and the case for nature in the chapters that follow, nature deserves independent treatment in order to illuminate the radical new ways in which flying, growing or swimming life forms are finally being valued. And in the small minority of cases where getting to net-zero emissions and building a nature-positive economy come into conflict – say, in mining minerals in ecologically sensitive areas, or siting transmission lines – I want both sides to get their due so that the trade-offs, where they arise, can be discussed honestly and resolved transparently.

With words that remain as relevant and chilling as they were in 1985, a speaker on the floor issued the following warning at a UN-organised public hearing in the years leading up to Rio. 'You talk very little about life,' they said. 'You talk too much about survival. It is very important to remember that when the possibilities for life are over, the possibilities for survival start. And there are peoples here in Brazil, especially in the Amazon region, who still live [...] [who] don't want to reach down to the level of survival.' [4]

Even if it were possible to geoengineer our way out of a warming planet while overseeing mass extinction in the natural world (which it isn't), those words remain instructive. For that outcome would offer us only survival, without life. The case for tackling climate change on its own is the case for ensuring human survival; the case for nature is, ultimately, the complementary case for securing a living planet worth living for.

The declarative nature of this book's title belies a certain complexity, for there are ultimately several sorts of cases for nature. Scholars far more qualified than I have explored the *economic* arguments for preserving nature and the notion of 'natural capital' for decades; activists and artists have made *intrinsic* cases for nature for centuries; spiritual traditions have arguably appealed to higher ideals in relation to nature for millennia. But each of these cases have, for too long, been viewed as separate – even as somehow in conflict with each other – when in fact they all form part of a powerful, indivisible case for nature.

Since I began researching this book in 2020, my own thinking has certainly evolved. I started with the assumption that the intrinsic arguments had been made well enough. I judged that they had reached a wide and increasingly receptive audience – a reflection, perhaps, of the environmentally conscious bubble I live and work in. Through hundreds of conversations, including with people who disagreed with me, I changed my mind: I came to view both motivations – economic *and* intrinsic – as deserving of far more attention.

To lay my own cards on the table: the intrinsic case on its own has always been more than powerful enough for me. I was raised by a family of conservationists in India, steeped in a culture that valued nature and the minimisation of ecological suffering, for its own sake. My grandmother and father spent years volunteering at the Blue Cross, nursing injured animals back to health; my mother later found her own way into conservation through her passion for wildlife photography. In researching this book, I was frequently reminded of the profoundly important and complementary need to cultivate love and respect for nature, and perhaps even a spiritual relationship to the natural world. Others have made that case persuasively through their writing, filmmaking and scholarship.

Having said all that, much of what follows nevertheless focuses on the economic case for nature.

For one, it is by far the less well-understood set of arguments, even in the green-tinged circles that I and perhaps you inhabit. Even as researchers and practitioners have plugged away at understanding the value of nature to human wellbeing for decades, the ideas underlying natural capital have only occasionally made the leap from academia and the NGO world to common parlance. Where they are discussed, as in the recent surge of interest in natural climate solutions, nature's utility is often viewed narrowly (say, in the planting of trees to draw down our carbon pollution). In pulling together a range of business cases, and describing them in accessible, jargon-light terms, I hope to bring the concept of natural capital to life as an integrated whole that is greater than the sum of its parts.

I also feel a sense of urgency that I cannot shake. The industrialised world, having pillaged for several centuries, now offers up to present and future generations a dangerously denuded set of landscapes and seascapes. But the task is even more urgent in the developing world: in countries like India and Indonesia, with growing populations that rightfully harbour economic aspirations. It's all very well to ask wealthy urban consumers to pay a premium for nature-friendly products. It's another thing entirely to expect the communities that live in, and typically steward, natural landscapes to give up their extractive routes to prosperity without enabling better ones in their place. What a tragedy it would be if they were forced to follow the same path as the West, belatedly atoning for their sins decades hence when tigers and Komodo dragons are but distant memories. If falling crop yields, historic floods and ever-more-frequent wildfires are warning signs these countries cannot choose to ignore, then models for restoration that also happen to make economic sense deserve attention, right now.

But, beyond the relative novelty and absolute urgency of the case for nature, what has made this book all the more enjoyable to write are the new possibilities offered by the technological and financial innovations I have come into contact with during my time as a student, entrepreneur and investor in this space. As we will see, we are now able to monitor ecosystems with incredible precision, creating the trust and transparency that all good markets are built on. We're refashioning the tools of high finance to channel funding into protection and restoration, rather than destruction. Investing in nature, for financial and social returns, is being made possible by these innovations; not all will achieve scale, but the energy and talent I encountered give me immense hope. This time feels different.

* * *

The chapters that follow dive into the many exciting ways in which this economic imperative for nature is finally coming to life. We'll see how the mangrove swamps of Colombia are helping us tackle climate change as we value their carbon services, how Fijian communities are protecting marine life through sustainable ecotourism, how farmers in Britain and elsewhere are demonstrating the ways in which the restoration of soil and ecosystem health can bring food security and assure livelihoods, and how cities across the world are becoming safer, cooler and more liveable by bringing nature in, rather than shutting it out.

In the past, such efforts might have run aground when it came to translating lofty ideals into tangible business models that can measure and value nature's contributions. Today, we have remarkable tools at our disposal that make this challenge eminently solvable; as well as the theory of natural capital, we'll also explore the technological and financial enablers that are bringing trust and scale to new environmental markets.

I haven't attempted to create a comprehensive list of global case studies as a textbook might. I was fortunate to be able to write opportunistically, learning along the way, each interview and field visit leading to more introductions and opportunities. Some chapters, like the one on ecotourism, naturally lent themselves to examination through the lens of (my own) personal experiences. Others, like the chapter on carbon markets, demanded a deeper dive into the scientific and technical details. In each chapter, I try to highlight different sides of the live debates that surround the various approaches and provide my own perspectives on them.

I should also clarify up front that the 'economic' or 'business' cases I refer to are not the exclusive preserve of businesses; as we will see, governments can and do invest in nature on behalf of their citizens, and typically make the public goods that emerge freely available to them. The point here is not private profit, but economic logic – the driving force that, for better or for worse, animates our economies and societies. In such a world, it remains my firm belief that nature deserves a seat at the financial table if we are to avoid relegating flora and fauna to a shrinking patchwork of protected areas at the fringes of the modern economy – museum pieces, in effect.

But economic logic, as widely applicable as it might be, can only go so far; each case builds on a set of underlying, intrinsic motivations to regenerate our long-suffering planet. Perhaps the chapter that gave me most cause for reflection and learning was the one on indigenous perspectives on nature. Having barely scratched the surface of the deep repository of wisdom that indigenous cultures hold, I began to see how tackling the biodiversity and climate crises would require a reconception of our very relationship with the planet. My research led me to rethink the framing of the entire book because I realised that this spiritual case for nature, rooted in deep time, is an important and egregiously overlooked part of the broader case for nature. I hope dearly that I have done it justice but remain humble about the limits of my own understanding and language, steeped as they are in the Western paradigm.

As you explore the array of cases in this book, I urge you to form and test your own perspectives. You might, for instance, end the journey with more conviction in the back-to-basics potential of regenerative agriculture than in the long-term integrity of carbon markets, more hope in the power of technology than in the promise of financial innovation to enable such shifts. On balance, I have come to believe in the potential of each of them, but I encourage you to treat this as a flavour of all that is out there, to bring a dose of healthy scepticism to everything you read in these pages and elsewhere, to continue exploring these themes through other books, papers and documentaries, and ultimately to make up your own mind. Whatever conclusion you come to, I hope you will leave better informed, more hopeful, and more motivated to make the case for nature in your own way.

I asked Christiana Figueres what lay behind her 'stubborn optimism' on our ability to tackle this emergency of our own making. 'What gives me hope is to see that, despite our stupid actions, we still have incredible resilience in nature. To see that the moment that we remove the pressure from nature, she tends to jump back,' she said with characteristic flair, reflecting on her native Costa Rica's journey to reversing deforestation and developing a thriving nature-based tourism economy as its wildlife populations rebounded. 'It's pretty amazing because nature could perfectly well have decided a long time ago that we are such idiots, she's just not going to tolerate us anymore. And the fact that she's still resilient is incredibly generous.'

Indeed. In the two years I spent researching this book, I found more reasons for optimism than I could possibly have imagined when I first set out. I'm delighted to be able to share them with you. Let's dive in.

A Natural Ally
in the Climate Fight

'Qué más?' Jhon asked, snapping his fingers over the sound of the engine. 'Has the Ciénaga's magic claimed you too?' As my host for the day steered our boat across the shimmering surface, I admitted to being lost in thought. We were on Colombia's stunning Caribbean coast, speeding into a vast wetland, water as far as the eye could see. My mind was wandering, reflecting on the variety of wondrous ecosystems that have earned this country a place on every nature lover's bucket list.

Colombia, positioned at the crossroads of the Americas, is home to the lush, tropical forest that makes up the western flank of the Amazon rainforest. Less well-known are the wind-swept, diverse Páramo grasslands high up in the Colombian Andes. 'Nowhere, perhaps, can be found collected together, in so small a space, productions so beautiful, and so remarkable in regard to the geography of plants,' Alexander von Humboldt, the great Prussian polymath and naturalist, once wrote of this ecosystem. Over 80 per cent of the species in the Páramo are endemic, seen nowhere else on earth.

I had now arrived at the sun-baked northern coast, where the mountains meet the sea and cloud forests are mere miles away from white-sand beaches. It is also where the Magdalena – the rushing river that runs the length of the country and has defined its history from pre-Columbian times – slows to a crawl before opening out into a vast patchwork of wetlands, marshes and mangrove forests.

I had come here to learn how these *ciénagas*, as the swamps are known, are playing a starring role in a new effort to harness carbon markets to fund nature's preservation and restoration.

Mangrove wetlands are tremendously carbon-rich: in addition to offering flood protection and a host of other eco-system benefits, their moist soils and trees lock up vast quantities of carbon. But the coastal land that mangroves occupy is typically highly prized. No wonder, then, that they have suffered the ravages of development the world over; Colombia's Caribbean coast is no exception.

Just two generations ago, these Caribbean wetlands were open to the sea; the estuarine waters teemed with life, and manatees and jaguars were not uncommon, as Wade Davis writes in *Magdalena*, his seminal and highly readable history of Colombia as seen through the lens of its largest river. Dozens of species of fish spawned in the mangroves, sheltered by their roots, before entering more open waters to provide a bountiful catch to fisherfolk like Jhon's forebears.

Then a perfect storm of capitalism and authoritarianism took hold in Colombia, bringing infrastructure development, intensive agriculture and logging that steadily ate away at the mangroves. In Cispata, to the west, the thick mangrove forests that once stood had been seriously degraded over a long period. But, as I drove east on the coastal highway to Santa Marta to meet Jhon, I noticed one very visible sign of what ailed these ecosystems. Passing Barranquilla, the highway turned into a two-lane strip of asphalt on what appeared to be a sand bank, flanked by vast expanses of water on either side. On the left, of course, was the sparkling Caribbean Sea. But on the right was the Ciénaga Grande de Santa Marta – the largest of the *ciénagas* – choked off from the ocean by the road.

The road had been built in the 1950s, turning an open tidal ecosystem into a hemmed-in lake. Banana plantations had later drawn off much of the fresh water, leaving tens of thousands of hectares of mangroves to wither away. The ducts built into the highway as an afterthought did little to restore the natural flow of water, and fish populations fell steadily over the decades. Glimmers of hope came in the late 1990s, when a torrential downpour flooded dams upriver and naturally restored some of the wetland; still, it was far from its former glory.

But even the degraded *Ciénaga* was stunningly beautiful and seemingly endless. An hour into our journey, we arrived in Buenavista and Nueva Venecia, two villages on stilts deep in the wetlands. We were greeted by the region's famed *cumbia* music, and by Zenit, a *mamo*, or matriarch, who remembered what the area had once been like.

'When I was a child, the water was so full of fish that all you had to do was dip your hands in the *ciénaga* to get your lunch!' she said. 'The mangroves still give us everything,' she added, gesturing at the floorboards of her house and the fish in her kitchen. 'I'd love to see them go back to the way they were when we were younger, but someone needs to pay for that! In the meantime, you can't blame us for trying to survive in any way we can.' Government schemes to pay for restoration had had some effect, but the programmes remained chronically underfunded.

Virtually everyone agrees that precious wetlands like these are critical for local communities, conservation and the wider climate. Cash-strapped national and regional governments have mostly fallen short. Private landowners, where they exist, often have other uses in mind for what is typically prime seafront property. And while many local and indigenous peoples are stewards of these ecosystems, who can blame them for making a living off the land?

Now, finally, carbon markets are beginning to value one ecosystem service that these mangroves provide: their ability to store carbon and stabilise the climate. In visiting Cispata, the world's first 'blue carbon' project, and the far-larger Ciénaga Grande, up the coast, I hoped to see first-hand what carbon markets had already started to do for the former, and the promise they held for the latter.

Carbon markets are far from perfect, as we will see. But they represent a real and increasingly viable entry point to pay for the protection and restoration of mangrove wetlands like the one I found myself in that morning, and the forests and grasslands that we cannot afford to lose. Carbon finance from global corporations and governments can, done right, create nature-positive livelihoods for local communities like Zenit's who are eager and willing to steward these landscapes, but who rightly demand the economic fruits of their labour.

Natural climate solutions are those that harness the remarkable climate-stabilising powers of nature. Studies estimate that the restoration of natural ecosystems could help absorb one-third of the global net emissions forecast for the years to 2050.[1] That ambitious goal would build on the tireless service that the world's terrestrial and ocean carbon sinks already provide when they absorb over 20 gigatonnes of carbon every year.[2] The climate crisis would be far more potent already if it were not for the planet's natural ability to buffer us from rising emissions.

But millennia of human activity have worn down the natural world. Archaeologists have found that humans had already transformed the planet through hunting, gathering and farming as far back as 3,000 years ago.[3] Such trends accelerated dramatically with the advent of colonialism and the industrial revolution; today, the WWF estimates that only a quarter of the world's landmass is largely free of human impacts, a figure set to shrink to 10 per cent by 2050 if current trends proceed apace.[4] We will have to reverse these trends and restore nature if we are to protect and expand Earth's innate ability to lock away carbon and moderate the global climate.

You might be forgiven for thinking that this potential for restoration is limited to tropical places like Colombia. Nothing could be further from the truth; if anything, the ecosystems of North America and Europe have fallen further from their ancient, wild states than anywhere else on Earth. The fact that the destruction happened earlier, and more comprehensively, should not mask the fact that these regions, too, hold incredible promise as natural carbon sinks.

We might like the idea of restoring nature, but isn't technological carbon capture a safer and in some ways more straightforward bet in the long term? Drawing down carbon can take many forms and it's true that technological solutions tend to be longer-lived – once carbon is stored geologically, it is unlikely to be re-released for hundreds or thousands of years.

There are a growing number of engineered solutions, including direct-air-capture machines that take carbon directly out of the atmosphere, and methods that rely on geological processes, such as the weathering of crushed rocks to capture carbon through chemical reaction with carbon dioxide in the atmosphere. There are also hybrid solutions that take natural biomass – like waste wood – and turn it into stable, long-lived carbon in the form of biochar or bio-oil with the help of pyrolysis technology.

But, while researchers and start-ups are working on a wide range of technology-based solutions, there is still a way to go before these are ready for widespread use. Direct air carbon capture, enhanced rock weathering, and the like are currently eye-wateringly expensive, costing as much as $500-$1,000 per tonne of CO_2 removed. While a few thousand tonnes have been captured and paid for, these solutions are far from achieving the gigatonne-level scale we need. It is in all our interests to invest in this technology now to drive down costs to manageable levels of perhaps $100 per tonne.

A range of innovative schemes, from advance commitments from companies like Stripe to purchase high-cost carbon removals, to generous tax credits like the ones in the US Inflation Reduction Act of 2022, are helping to kickstart this market. But we remain at least a decade, and perhaps two, away from achieving lower costs and meaningful volumes. Nothing illustrates this better than the ambitious stretch goal that Climeworks, a leading direct-air-capture company, has set itself: to capture a million tonnes by 2030. Getting there, from the 4,000 tonnes the company's first plant in Iceland could capture annually in 2022, will take billions of dollars of investment and a series of engineering breakthroughs.

While it can be tempting to see technology and nature as at odds with each other, the reality is that, given the urgency and scale of the task at hand, we need both ends of that spectrum and everything in between.

We cannot simply wait for technological solutions to scale up. Thankfully, we already have a way to draw down carbon and lock it away for decades, if not centuries, at a tiny fraction of their current price tag. The planet's natural ecosystems – its forests, wetlands and grasslands – are our best allies, at least in the short term, as we race to limit catastrophic climate change. The numbers are staggering: the Cispata pilot project alone is set to remove one million tonnes of carbon in its thirty-year project lifetime.[5]

In the rest of this chapter, I largely discuss climate solutions that protect and restore ecosystems. I do so not to diminish the immense potential of technological carbon removal, but in order to focus on the solutions that can drive action on climate and nature in parallel. I want to show that the business case for investing in our ecosystems today is a powerful one, even as we continue placing bold bets on transformative technologies that we hope to rely on in future decades.

Let's look in more detail at carbon markets to understand how they can help finance our ecosystem protection and restoration goals. These markets – mechanisms that allow the trading of credits (units of carbon reduction or removal) – evolved in response to the sobering reality of the climate challenge. The world now emits the equivalent of 52 billion tonnes of CO_2 every year.[6] Carbon dioxide is to blame for about two-thirds of that figure, with the rest accounted for by methane and other greenhouse gases. Even the Covid-19 pandemic made only a small dent in that figure; emissions of CO_2-equivalents (CO_2e) dropped around 7 per cent in 2020, but quickly rebounded to the pre-crisis trend in 2021. We know the world needs to move to 'net-zero' carbon emissions by 2050, or ideally sooner, to avoid catastrophic climate change. Unfortunately, the UN Emissions Gap report makes clear that we're simply not on track.[7] Greenhouse gas emissions are set to rise to 59 gigatonnes by 2030 if we continue with business as usual. Big changes will have to be made to strip out carbon emissions from the ways in which we make things, move around, and feed the world.

Net zero is the aim, but that doesn't mean we have to get to absolute zero carbon emissions across the economy (an even taller order that few believe is feasible). While scientists and entrepreneurs are racing to decarbonise vast swathes of the economy, from electricity generation to transport, there will likely always be some emissions that are too challenging, or too expensive, to avoid entirely. In a net-zero world in 2050, there may still be emissions from long-distance aviation or cement production that are yet to be fully decarbonised.

Minimising emissions wherever we can is an urgent, essential task, but the remaining fraction will need to be balanced out by drawing carbon out of the atmosphere and locking it away in carbon sinks.

This is where carbon offsets come into the picture, both now and for that future net-zero world. For every tonne of CO_2e emitted, it should, in theory, be possible to compensate elsewhere. After all, carbon dioxide, unlike some other forms of pollution, disperses all over the world once it's emitted. A tonne of carbon dioxide emitted from a coal-fired power plant in, say, Texas will enter the Earth's atmosphere and hang around for centuries, resulting in a specific amount of additional warming potential. Methane, on the other hand, is far more potent, but doesn't stay in the atmosphere quite as long. Scientists compare the different gases that add to the greenhouse effect in CO2-equivalents, or CO2e, rating their contribution to warming against that representative tonne of CO2. So, a tonne of methane released from a dairy farm in Wales would represent roughly 25 tonnes of CO2e, which we can then use to compare to the damages caused by the Texas smokestack.

Polluters, be they dairy farms or tech companies, can compensate for their emissions in two ways. They can pay to avoid equivalent emissions that would otherwise have occurred (**avoided emissions**) or to support the physical draw-down of greenhouse gases directly from the atmos-phere (carbon **removals**).

Both are vitally important. Deforestation alone accounts for about 10 per cent of global greenhouse gas emissions, as trees are cut down or burned and formerly rich forest soils dry out and lose carbon. We need to take new emissions from deforestation and landscape degradation down to zero, urgently, and money that can make that happen in the absence of perfect government regulation is surely welcome.

But it's also true that in a net-zero world, we'll need to be drawing down actual new tonnes of carbon to balance those last few tonnes of unavoidable emissions. It won't be enough just to avoid future emissions from deforestation and the like; we will need to restore formerly active carbon sinks and create new ones. As we'll see later in the chapter, it helps to do two things to cut through the complexity of carbon markets. First, focus on the supply side, to ensure that the impacts on the ground are real, credible and beneficial for nature and communities. Second, encourage actors on the demand side, usually large companies, to compensate for their unavoidable emissions only through high-quality credits, where rigorous claims can be made about impact, while continuing to seek out and cut their avoidable emissions aggressively in parallel.

While the science behind nature-based carbon sequestration is getting better by the day, the art of packaging these actions up into trustworthy credits, and getting paid for them, is just as important.

Think of the distinction we made just above between *avoidance* and *removal* credits. Historically, the majority of nature-based credits have been of the former type: paying to protect reasonably healthy ecosystems that might otherwise be at risk, rather than actively restoring fallow or degraded land. How do we know the carbon impacts – perhaps from protecting a forest or restoring a grassland – have actually occurred? Both types of credits need to be verified, typically by third parties. The developers of credits can sign up to any of the several sets of standards that are widely in use, with each entitling them to access different 'markets' for these credits across the world.

These markets can broadly be split in two. The first set, called **compliance** markets, have been set up by governments or international bodies to incentivise decarbonisation. The European Union and the State of California have, for instance, set up cap-and-trade schemes where big emitters like power plants and steelworks are given annual emissions allocations. These caps are set to incentivise companies to lower emissions – by switching to cleaner fuels or scrubbing the gases that leave their smokestacks. If they stay below the annual carbon cap, which shrinks with time, these companies pay nothing. But it doesn't always work that way; emitters sometimes find these caps too expensive or technically challenging to meet. That's where the *trading* part of a cap-and-trade system comes in. Compliance markets allow polluters to make amends by buying allowances from other entities that have achieved steeper-than-expected cuts. Carbon pricing schemes like this one, or carbon taxes like those in South Africa or Sweden, have spread to dozens of countries, and played a role in regulating nearly a quarter of global emissions in 2020.[8] Not all of them allow emitters to buy nature-based credits, but some do. The EU, for instance, doesn't allow nature-based credits to substitute for allowances; regulated entities in the California market can offset a small proportion (4–6 per cent) of their emissions by buying certified forest credits instead.[9]

If compliance markets can be seen as brakes on the big, old polluters of the energy economy, **voluntary** markets have sprung up to serve a different set of buyers. From individuals seeking to offset the impact of their flying, to large corporations seeking to undo the carbon impact of their electricity use or travel, voluntary markets, small as they currently are, have been an important catalyst for nature-based climate solutions. Administered by non-profit bodies such as Verra, Gold Standard or the American Carbon Registry, these rely on a network of independent third-party verifiers to ensure that reductions actually occur.

So how much does a carbon credit cost? In traded compliance markets, credits should really be referred to as allowances (given the mandatory nature of the caps), and pricing is typically determined as it would be on a stock exchange. Buyers and sellers exchange credits, and prices rise or fall based on demand – subject, of course, to any floor prices that governments might set to ensure carbon prices don't fall too low during recessions or periods of market volatility. In mid-2022, the price of regulated allowances in the European Union's emissions trading scheme hovered between €80–90, having risen strongly from around €25 at the end of 2020.

The voluntary market is a bit more of a wild west even if governments across the world are beginning to regulate them as the voluntary and compliance markets become more integrated. For now, buyers and sellers exchange offsets either directly, or through a network of intermediaries that spans the globe. Prices can be negotiated by project or credits can be packaged up into a portfolio and sold on. Nature-based offset prices in these markets averaged around $10 per tonne in mid-2022 but can be as high as $20–40 per tonne if they offer *removals*, rather than *avoided emissions*, or create 'co-benefits' such as biodiversity or jobs for local communities. The prices of both types of credits have grown from the low-to-mid single-digits back in 2020.

If this still sounds cheap, that's because it is. Nature, even at the upper end of that range, offers carbon sequestration at somewhere between a tenth and a fiftieth of the current cost of technological carbon capture. Carbon markets can channel valuable money into funding conservation in some of the poorest and/or most biodiverse parts of the world. As with everything, though, you get what you pay for – as we'll see when we explore the all-too-real issues with quality in the second half of this chapter.

Carbon markets can seem like an abstract and oddly techno-cratic solution to the real, hyper-local challenges of protecting and restoring ecosystems. Indeed, the work needed to set up one of these projects is as hands-on as you might expect, combining field studies with community engagement and long-term project management. Carbon markets ultimately help pay for all this activity to take place, but the most rigor-ous projects, like the one I visited in Colombia, make sure to involve a range of stakeholders from the very beginning.

In Colombia, the backers of the carbon project began in the mangrove wetlands of Cispata. The pilot scheme, dubbed Vida Manglar ('Mangrove Life'), brought together local commu-nities and the government; NGOs, including Conservation International; INVEMAR, the coastal research agency; and tech giant Apple.

The scientific team had their work cut out for them. How do you measure the carbon stored in a wetland? For trees, the work is usually easier. We have good models, refined over decades, for the carbon stored in wood above ground. In wetlands, a lot of the carbon is stored underground – in those rich, silty soils, held together by mangroves, grasses and their endlessly branching root networks. Scientists trudged through the swamps, extracting soil three metres deep at various sites and sending them back to labs to be studied. They concluded that up to four-fifths of all the natural carbon in the wetland was underground, and essentially underwater, handily justifying the 'blue carbon' moniker that is applied to climate solutions in wetlands, coastal areas and the open ocean.

Restoring and protecting the Cispata wetland – a small fraction of the broader ecosystem – was set to remove a million tonnes of atmospheric CO_2 over thirty years. And that's where carbon markets came in, packaging up those future emissions reductions as carbon credits and selling them to individuals or companies that wanted to offset the emissions they were unable to avoid.

A team surveys the degraded Cispata wetland in Colombia. © Daniel Uribe, by permission.

Mangrove restoration gets underway in Cispata. ©
María Claudia Diazgranados, by permission.

Paula Sierra of INVEMAR, the coastal research institute that had carried out the scientific work for the pilot
project, helped design the project in partnership with those
who called the wetland home. 'We were thrilled to see how
enthusiastic and supportive the local communities were,
and we created good, well-paying jobs while protecting a
critical ecosystem.' These jobs included the physical work of
restoring the area's hydrology, the community engagement
work that helped reduce deforestation, and the monitoring
work over time. Government schemes in the protected area
were also now better funded, she told me. 'Carbon credits
have been a lifeline and have nearly doubled the agency's
restoration budget.'

Other carbon projects, in varied ecosystems from Peruvian forests to Tanzanian savannah, have taken similar steps to funnel money back into communities in the form of education and healthcare or infrastructure funding; the proportion of carbon credit revenue that actually gets paid out to communities in the form of jobs, community schemes, or cash, can be a helpful proxy for the degree of local engagement and buy-in. This is, after all, a question of economic development as much as it is one of ecology.

A few months after my trip, Conservation International announced that all the credits from the Cispata site had been sold, with over 92 per cent of the proceeds going into the project's conservation plan and local communities.[10] But Cispata was just the start; Paula and her colleagues were already dreaming bigger. 'The Ciénaga Grande is over twenty times the size of Cispata. If that first project could create one million tonnes of carbon benefits, just imagine what we could do if we scale this up across the coast.'

Carbon Credits

Carbon markets can help value and enhance natural carbon storage, but how do we know **what makes a good credit?** What criteria can we use to ascertain that a credit represents a real, measurable unit of carbon avoided or removed that can help offset unavoidable emissions? *(Read the following section if you want to equip yourself with the tools to separate the wheat from the chaff – or feel free to skip ahead for now and return to it later.)*

The first criterion is **additionality,** to show that a carbon project has gone above and beyond business-as-usual. Simply put, additionality captures the degree to which a carbon credit has incentivised action that wouldn't otherwise have occurred. A related notion is the baseline – our best guess of what would have occurred in the absence of a credit; establishing this counterfactual allows us to judge the impact of a carbon project.

For *avoidance* projects, baselines can be particularly tricky to establish. How are we to know what would have happened to a standing forest in the absence of the project? In such cases, developers and verifiers need to make a conservative forecast of what deforestation would have occurred. A conservative baseline forecast might assume some improvement on general deforestation over the coming decade, compare forests elsewhere that are not enrolled in credit programmes, or introduce additional variables like crop or timber prices that can often predict future rates of deforestation.

Baselines for carbon *removal* projects are more straightforward. Developers typically look at land that has, for decades, been intensively farmed or deforested and abandoned. Removals projects then involve paying land stewards to store carbon in trees (via reforestation or agroforestry) or in the soil (through regenerative agriculture).

In any case, supported by new technologies the field is moving towards dynamic, rather than fixed, baselines, based on what actually takes place in surrounding areas as time goes on.

The next thing to look for is **leakage**, in order to be reasonably certain that project is actually stopping destruction, rather than simply shifting – that is, leaking – it elsewhere to nearby sites that lack protection.

Beyond working closely with local and national policymakers, the other way to tackle leakage is to zoom out. Loggers and miners might be able to get away with moving their destruction to other parts of the same locality or province, but this activity would still be detected if we look at deforestation rates across entire *jurisdictions*. 'Jurisdictional' credits are distinct from project-based ones: in principle, they reward progress across entire states or countries, with the benefits being shared across governments, private developers and civil society. Individual projects can be 'nested' within a jurisdictional approach to ensure coordination between local action and national ambition. There are still important questions to be worked out at the international level on jurisdictional credits, but they represent one way forward to reduce the risk of leakage.

Again, leakage is less of a concern when dealing with restoration projects; paying to replant a degraded mangrove is unlikely to shift destruction elsewhere, since the degradation has already occurred.

Third, we need to make a judgement on the durability of carbon drawdown, also known as **permanence**.

No ecosystem is truly permanent on geological time-scales. But we don't have to worry about million-year timescales just yet; we have a far more pressing problem that needs solving now. As we figure out how to scale permanent technological carbon capture and storage, we really need natural means in the next two decades, and perhaps through the end of the century, to avoid imminent catastrophe.

Ten-, thirty- or one-hundred-year periods are the most common promises that forest or soil projects make on durability. In addition to securing community buy-in, developers typically guarantee durability by setting up legal structures, such as long-term land leases and contracts with terms that secure a newly restored ecosystem for a defined period. Some have sought to do away with long-term contracts, instead calculating how many years of temporary storage of carbon are essentially equivalent to 'permanent' sequestration. The jury is still out, but this sort of 'tonne–year' accounting is already being used for projects like the one that carbon market startup NCX runs to persuade foresters to defer timber harvests and store more carbon in their trees.

What about other risks that can't be contracted away, like the threat of wildfires? Carbon projects insure against unexpected losses by setting aside a proportion of credits (typically 10–20 per cent) in a 'buffer pool'. Buffer pools can't account for total losses, so some ecosystems, like the wildfire-prone forests of the Western United States, may be inappropriate for 100-year carbon projects. In parallel, insurers are dipping their toes in the voluntary carbon market to help protect buyers. Finally, a portfolio approach can diversify risk.

Nature is a dynamic system. Ecosystems grow, shrink and change over the years – it's all part of the ecological flux. What matters is that real dollars should take carbon out of the atmosphere and begin cycling it through the food web at meaningful scales. If, decades from now, natural carbon sequestration ends up being superseded by technological carbon capture, that will still leave us with dynamic natural ecosystems that will be worth protecting for the many other benefits they bring.

Finally, we need to **monitor** and **verify** carbon projects to make sure that promises are kept.

How can we trust that credits are additional and permanent? The same way we do when we're asked to trust that a company's accounts are honest – by turning to auditors who ensure that their conditions are met. In the voluntary market, natural carbon credits are typically certified by one of several non-profit organisations that set standards, like Verra or the American Carbon Registry. Credits that hope to enter government-run markets like California's must meet their respective standards too.

If the process sounds complex, it is. As a result, fixed costs can be high, and traditional verification methods don't provide real-time or high-frequency data. Thankfully, as we will explore later, we're beginning to develop new monitoring hardware along with vastly improved datasets and software that can complement the army of in-field nature auditors. These tools will allow us to verify with unprecedented levels of confidence that ecosystems are being managed and restored as planned.

Finally, an emerging class of independent entities is helping keep verifiers honest, much like Human Rights Watch or Reporters Without Borders in their respective arenas. CarbonPlan, one such non-profit focused on carbon market research, has produced independent assessments of offset transactions including those of Microsoft and Stripe. There is more to be done: 'Today's private markets are not supplying the level of disclosure required to fully vet these efforts, which makes screening more difficult and expensive for those seeking quality outcomes,' the organisation says.[11] As the market forges ahead, efforts like CarbonPlan's are boosting independent verification capability and transparency.

If carbon markets are such a good idea, and we know what we're looking for, what's holding them back? Critics have asked important questions; now let's examine some of these challenges and the ways in which they are being overcome.

Can we really trust carbon credits?

Trust must be earned. Unfortunately, the nature-based credit market hasn't always done a great job of building trust on the additionality, leakage, permanence and verification metrics. Early nature-based credits schemes were critiqued for paying for forest protection in places such as Cambodia and India but failing to monitor projects as they came under pressure from logging and agriculture. Some were certified under the UN's well-intentioned but nonetheless flawed Reducing Emissions from Deforestation and Forest Degradation (UN-REDD) framework, where implementation loopholes and a lack of monitoring capacity collectively eroded trust.

Beyond ignoring the outright destruction of forests that were earmarked for protection, avoided emissions projects have also come under scrutiny for setting unrealistic baselines. Conservation groups and national governments have, at various points, claimed carbon credits on areas of pristine forest that already benefitted from protection under the law.

It's worth noting that price, additionality, leakage and durability are often correlated. The least additional projects – the ones that are cheapest and set the dodgiest baselines, for instance – are often the ones that are least likely to represent durable, high-quality carbon impacts.

These past mistakes should serve as cautionary tales. Thankfully, today's improved credits are proving that a better way is possible. For a start, leading voluntary credit certifiers have tightened their criteria, and instituted more frequent monitoring, to improve trust in the system. New bodies such as the Integrity Council and the Voluntary Carbon Markets Integrity Initiative have been set up to bring stakeholders together and create consensus on higher standards.

Spurred on by an agreement on an international emissions trading rulebook at the COP26 climate summit, certification schemes are moving towards 'jurisdictional' approaches that embed credits within broader national climate goals. The LEAF coalition, launched at the 2021 Climate Leaders' Summit by the UK, the US and Norway, uses a stringent new jurisdictional standard for tropical forest protection, with dozens of states and countries now in exploratory talks. In both contexts, deforestation baselines are being set in a much more conservative, data-driven way. Meanwhile, interest in removal projects, which do not suffer from the same baseline issues, is gaining steam.

Importantly, sophisticated buyers are beginning to acknowledge that not all credits are equal, even in this vastly improved new world. Large private purchasers are doing their own research on projects, weeding out laggards and helping to raise standards across the board.

The system is still far from perfect. But coming under the microscope of journalists and activists over the last decade has been a good thing for scrupulous sellers, discerning buyers, and the planet. Trust is, slowly but surely, being built.

Aren't carbon credits just a get-out-of-jail-free card for polluters?

Critics of carbon offsetting argue that they offer polluting companies and jet-setting individuals a free pass. Why bother trying to reduce emissions when they can simply offset them? This is not a trivial concern, but a compelling combination of public pressure and technological progress is helping to assuage it. Principled buyers everywhere are proving that it is possible to make dramatic cuts in carbon emissions while simultaneously catalysing a market for high-quality natural carbon credits and verifying them rigorously along the way.

Microsoft is one such buyer. The company began by setting an internal carbon price of $15 per tonne, charging departments for emissions from air travel and the like. The proceeds, and additional funds, have been reinvested in clean energy and zero-waste projects; by 2025, all direct power purchases will be from renewable sources. Microsoft's servers are becoming ever-more-efficient, as are its buildings.

Microsoft calls itself 'carbon neutral' today, but acknowledges the limitations of that term. 'Like most carbon-neutral companies, Microsoft has achieved carbon neutrality primarily by investing in offsets that avoid emissions instead of removing carbon that has already been emitted. That's why we're shifting our focus. In short, neutral is not enough to address the world's need,' the company admitted in 2020, adding that 'while it is imperative that we continue to avoid emissions, and these investments remain important, we see an acute need to begin removing carbon from the atmosphere, which we believe we can help catalyse through our investments'.[12] Since then, Microsoft has led the way in setting a decarbonisation target with the Science-Based Targets Initiative, a framework through which businesses can seek to align their emissions with a 1.5°C pathway.[13] Having already achieved deep cuts in direct emissions, it has also committed to going carbon-negative by 2030 – which means the company will physically remove more carbon than it emits by purchasing removal credits.

Microsoft has already begun to support the burgeoning carbon market by purchasing a portfolio of high-quality removal credits across a range of project types. By transparently publishing all proposals and purchases, and going public with the lessons it learnt along the way, Microsoft is leading the way in showing that credits can be valuable tools in the fight against climate change, rather than a free pass for carbon pollution.[14]

We'll need to keep the pressure up to ensure more companies take an approach like Microsoft's; we'll essentially need to set up guardrails for companies that constitute the 'demand' side of the market, in addition to 'supply' side efforts to raise the integrity of credits themselves. Doing so will require us to distinguish between companies setting science-based targets and following through on them, and those that might be seeking to greenwash their image by investing in low-quality credits. The claims companies make are important, particularly when buying natural carbon credits that avoid, rather than remove, carbon. Rather than calling themselves 'carbon neutral', they might choose to make more nuanced claims – perhaps they are 'compensating' for emissions, or 'supporting ecosystem stewards'. Carbon removals might allow for a stronger claim to be 'neutralising' emissions. The distinction between terms like compensation and neutralisation might seem almost vanishingly fine but language matters. Precision is a good thing for buyers themselves because it can head off criticisms of greenwashing. We also need radical transparency to build trust across the system. Scrutiny is no bad thing. There will always be those who object to carbon markets on principle, but many critics of subpar credits are providing a valuable service to the planet. Welcoming and acting on constructive criticism will only help strengthen carbon markets. Either way, the only credible buyers are the ones that can demonstrate that they are doing all they can to *cut* internal and supply-chain emissions.

Buyers that use credits as only one tool in their toolkits deserve our support. The greenwashers rightly deserve the bad press they get. Lumping them all together serves no one – and certainly not the priceless ecosystems that could badly use those carbon dollars.

Buyers should always aim higher, particularly when in positions of privilege. On a personal level, I double-offset my own emissions with a portfolio of high-quality natural carbon removal credits. I do so partly to quiet the ever-present seed of doubt in my mind over whether each credit really represents a full tonne of carbon dioxide, but mainly in the knowledge that overshooting is no bad thing. Governments and companies should feel obliged to go beyond the bare minimum, and perhaps even begin drawing down their historical carbon footprints in addition to cutting present and future emissions.

Are carbon projects environmentally just? Do local and indigenous communities share the benefits?

Environmental justice – ensuring that financial and other benefits are shared equitably – is a vitally important dimension to consider when making any sort of business case for nature.

Many forest carbon projects in the early 2000s failed to adequately consult local and indigenous communities, provoking understandable backlash and a sense that unnamed global actors were taking advantage of marginalised groups. The onus must be on those with the power to ensure that all stakeholders are brought into these projects and share in the dividends. Indeed, such efforts can ensure the longevity of projects and help bolster claims of permanence.

The Vida Manglar team, for instance, worked closely with local leaders to put in place a transparent benefit-sharing system. In exchange, the communities agreed to divide the area into twenty-three blocks and implement a rotational system of sustainable exploitation, so each block had a decade or more to recover from logging. Zero logging would of course be ideal for the ecosystem but preserving community rights to low-impact use is one important element of sustainable carbon projects – even if it means fewer credits are generated as a result.

Increasingly, high-integrity project developers are taking a community-centric approach, conscious as they are of the growing calls for environmental justice in carbon markets. Local communities are increasingly leading carbon projects themselves, as we'll see later when we explore how Kenya's Maasai are securing their lands by means of technology and carbon finance. By devoting the majority of carbon revenue to community enhancement and engaging local stakeholders to decide how that money gets spent, carbon developers are cultivating the humility and patience that they will need to avoid the pitfalls of the first wave of carbon projects.

Having failed to value nature for centuries, carbon markets offer us a promising pathway to correcting a market failure of planetary proportions. So, for all the inherent complexity of natural ecosystems, we can't afford to let perfect be the enemy of the good. As we've seen, the cheapest credits represent little more than empty promises; the best ones are making a meaningful difference in the places that matter. The latter might not be perfect, but they represent our best hope of achieving the large-scale carbon drawdown we need over the next decade.

We'll need to broaden our approach to nature-based offsets to deliver the supply required to meet soaring demand. First, looking beyond forest carbon, we can tap into the tremendous potential of agroforestry, mangroves and other aquatic eco-systems, which are currently marginal players in the carbon markets. We'll also need to shift our focus from avoided emis-sions to natural removals and view the former as a bridge to the latter. For purchasers, this might mean taking a punt on newer project types that incentivise further investment in this space. Public and philanthropic money could help to bridge the gap between more mature sectors, like forest carbon, and nascent areas of the market, like blue carbon in the deep sea.

A note of caution: the governments and communities that are beginning to see real money flow into nature should not treat carbon revenue as perpetual. The truth is no one really knows yet how carbon markets will evolve, and they might wax and wane over the coming decades, depending on what else is happening in the climate fight. Instead, these entities need to use the money to put in place legal protections, transition economic systems to more sustainable models, raise living standards, and make physical improvements (restoring hydrology in wetlands, for instance) that will long outlast the projects themselves.

Nature-based carbon credits are no silver bullet; we'll need a suite of strategies and alternative economic models to stem the destruction of our natural ecosystems, as we'll see throughout this book. Not all ecosystems are suited to the additionality or baseline tests that create high-quality carbon credits – forests that aren't at risk of deforestation, for instance, still merit investment through some other mechanism, like results-based finance or foreign aid. But carbon markets represent the clearest vindication of the essential logic underlying the economic case for nature.

As more stakeholders reckon with their role in fuelling the climate emergency, nature's climate-stabilising powers are finally being valued. Each (high-quality) credit sold represents an investment to secure and expand that value.

Who can blame Zenit of Nueva Venecia for having turned to the forest to feed and shelter her family, or the Colombian government for having failed to find the tax revenue to protect every last ecosystem among competing demands? Carbon markets could now offer them an economically viable path to protection, complemented over time with other cases for nature, such as ecotourism or sustainable aquaculture, in Cispata, Cienaga Grande and beyond.

If – and this is a big if – we can get them right, carbon markets could be one building block of a new paradigm for twenty-first-century conservation: one that no longer simply relies on charity or noble sacrifice from those who can least afford it, but instead creates livelihoods and buy-in among those who richly deserve to be rewarded for their long-overlooked stewardship of our vital ecosystems.

A Rough Guide
to Ecotourism

The tiny Twin Otter plane swooped low over emerald-green forests and turquoise lagoons, and our pilots appeared in no rush to get to their destination. After two long, hard years sealed off from the world, who could blame them? As 2021 drew to a close, Fiji was finally open, and everyone seemed to have taken on the role of impromptu welcome party, simply glad to be able to show off their island nation to the world once more.

The very name, Fiji, had evoked in my mind that mid-century notion of a paradise both pristine and remote. In truth, Fiji had long ceased to be particularly inaccessible. Commercial tourism began in the 1960s, and over half a million tourists were arriving in Fiji every year by the turn of the millennium. Until, of course, the pandemic sent Fiji back into true isolation of a sort it had not experienced in a century. In the dying days of 2021, the country's tourism economy

– which indirectly supports one third of Fiji's workforce – had sputtered back to life after a successful vaccination campaign.

The journey on a rickety propeller-plane to the eastern island of Taveuni had shown us some of Fiji's natural riches from the air, but I was looking forward to exploring Fiji's underwater life – the reefs and marine life that made it one of the world's top destinations for divers and marine conservationists. I had come here to see how responsible, community-centred, ecological tourism could offer a powerful case for nature.

The notion that tourism can be linked to conservation is at least as old as Yellowstone, established as the world's first national park in 1872. The Yellowstone Act envisioned a 'public pleasuring-ground' for all Americans – though this framing did not include the Native Americans who had inhabited these same lands for centuries, and had been violently excluded to make way for settlers and conservationists alike. Back then, conservation was also synonymous with game hunting, and many early conservationists like Theodore Roosevelt saw no contradiction between their love for nature and a relentless desire to conquer it with guns and crossbows.

Nature-inclined visitors began to trickle in, helped along by organisations like The Sierra Club, a conservation group founded in the United States in 1892. A key part of their appeal to the general public were annual wilderness excursions starting in 1901, when the first Sierra Club 'High Trip' took ninety-six members on an excursion to Yosemite National Park with the aim of turning tourists into advocates for conservation.

These early shoots of ecotourism were coming up against a backdrop of rising interest in tourism of all sorts. In the centuries prior, travel for the sake of it had remained off-limits to all but the very wealthiest. But as incomes rose following the industrial revolution, people began to move – even as examples of early 'over-tourism' in places like Brighton began to prophesy what was to come. [1,2]

Global tourism as we know it today really took off in the mid-twentieth century when flying transformed travel forever. Starting first in Europe and America, and later in Asia and the rest of the world, people began to roam for pleasure. Travel became cheaper and easier than it had ever been in human history.

At the heart of many conceptions of tourism – and the marketing campaigns that fuelled its popularity – is the notion of paradise free of human influence. But as simplistic and Western-centric as that notion always was, mass tourism by the 1970s had begun to represent a grave threat even to these supposed pockets of paradise. In parallel, the risks of cultural erasure grew, particularly where tourism brought outsiders in contact with indigenous peoples – though tourism's impact paled in comparison to commercial incursions for logging, hunting, mining and the like.

*   *   *

In 1976, a century after the opening of Yellowstone, Gerardo Budowksi suggested the potential for a symbiotic relationship between tourism and conservation as he surveyed the environmental damage that mass tourism had wrought in the decades prior.[3] Could a gentler, more thoughtful form of travel – ecotourism – offer an antidote? Rather than being detrimental to nature, perhaps tourism could be employed as a viable tool to fund conservation and inspire wider eco-consciousness.

This apparent win–win idea gradually took hold: in 1982, the term 'ecotourism' was added to the Oxford English Dictionary, that reliable marker of the mainstream, and the UN declared 2002 the International Year of ecotourism. In the decades since, responsible travel has only grown as a phenomenon. It's not hard to see why; the idea that travel can be a force for good is a seductive one.

But as with any environmental innovation, greenwashing abounded, and the ecotourism moniker was applied far more broadly than it should have been. It turned out that the dictionary definition was far from sufficient – delineating genuine ecotourism remains a challenge to this day.

To be clear, even self-declared ecotourism remains niche. While the broader tourism market was estimated to be worth $1.8 trillion in 2019, less than 10 per cent of that was accounted for by ecotourism.[4, 5] Still, it is now one of the fastest-growing sectors in the travel industry, with surveys pointing to growing interest in more sustainable travel.[6]

Why are we talking about something so seemingly outdated as tourism, set against the innovation taking place in carbon markets and technology? The truth is that for many places (or entire countries, as is the case in Fiji) ecotourism remains the most tangible business case for nature there is.

In short, money and jobs matter. That $180 billion, ecotourism's share of the overall market, is roughly 180 times the dollar-value of the voluntary carbon market in 2021.[7] By a broader measure of nature-based tourism, protected areas hosted eight billion visitors before the pandemic, generating $600 billion in income.[8]

Tourism of this sort creates jobs. The World Travel and Tourism Council put direct employment from 'wildlife tourism' at 9.1 million just before the pandemic, with at least twice as many employed indirectly.[9] In light of ecotourism's vast (and growing) relevance, it's worth learning the lessons of the past and working to get it right for the future.

Our port of call at the end of that first flight was Viani Bay, tucked away on the eastern spur of Fiji's second island, Vanua Levu. There are no roads in or out of the horseshoe bay; all of its roughly 100 residents trek over the surrounding hills on foot, or motor in and out by boat. We chose the latter, skipping over the waves from the airstrip on nearby Taveuni island at first light, a flood of moonlight giving way to vermilion, orange, and sapphire-blue skies in quick succession.

I suspected the long journey would be worth it. Viani, after all, is perfectly situated for divers looking to access Fiji's famed Rainbow Reef, first mapped by Jacques Cousteau and one of the world's prime examples of the soft-coral ecosystem. In normal times, the reef would be teeming not just with fish, but with visitors from across the world. But in these early days of Fiji's tentative post-pandemic reopening, we had this bucket-list dive site virtually to ourselves.

The resort I was visiting in Viani Bay, a small, three-bungalow operation called Dive Academy Fiji, is the brainchild of Marina Walser and Jone Waitaiti, business partners who met on Germany's frigid (and, in my mind, utterly inexplicable) scuba-diving circuit. Marina, tired of a long career in the corporate world, had wanted a change of scenery that involved better weather and diving; Jone had yearned to return to his native Fiji.

The journey from dream to reality was a long one. Camping on the beach for nearly a year, they worked with local trades-people to put up their wooden bungalows, in the traditional Fijian *bure* style. Slowly winning the trust of the community, they developed a successful, sustainable dive operation that lasted three years. Then the pandemic hit and Fiji shut down, forcing them to survive on hosting local visitors and the occasional yacht. During the lockdown period, many of

Fiji's over 100,000 tourism workers returned to their villages, making ends meet through farming, fishing, and government relief. While many workers in the rest of the world moved online to do business, many Fijians quite literally went back to their roots. Ecotourism operators, and their conservation efforts too, had to survive on public funding and the hope that visitors would eventually return.

We were the first group to arrive since the big reopening, and what the resort lacked in outright luxury it more than made up for with personal touches. For one, there was the food: seasonal, locally sourced and tailored to guests' dietary preferences. Our plant-based diets seemed to pose no problem, and we quickly became acquainted with the scandalously overlooked delights of Fijian cuisine. Generous meals featured taro, breadfruit, pumpkin and Fijian spinach, interspersed with Indian-influenced soups and curries seasoned with local fleur de sel and wild chillies. Coconut-milk ice cream was a regular, welcome feature, cutting as it did through the summer heat.

All the more remarkable was that these beautifully pre-sented dishes were prepared not by professional chefs from the big city, but by women recruited and trained locally in tiny Viani Bay, most of whom had never before been in formal employment. The same ethos of opportunity for the community animated the dive operation: the dive guides, knowledgeable and meticulous, were from local fishing families and had received scholarships that covered the cost of their certification as dive masters.

Life was simple in Viani, dictated by the rhythms of sun and sea. Each morning, we rose early, and the guides pored over tide charts to pick out the day's sites. This patient approach yielded fabulous results: plunging in just as a nutrient-rich current roared to life after two days of quieter seas, we saw the Great White Wall of soft coral in full bloom and swam through eerie forests of sea fans. With firm limits on artificial lighting to avoid disturbing the island's fauna, we'd retreat to our cabins by sunset, to be in bed by nine and up at sunrise ready to dive again.

The Rainbow Reef is not immune from the pressures of warming seas and overfishing that afflict reefs across the world. The 2014–2016 El Niño hit the South Pacific particularly hard, but I was glad to see Fiji's reefs bouncing back. The ghost-town effects of coral bleaching were mostly in retreat, and the vivid colours of the coral and the fish shone through the blue.

Conservation-minded operators like Marina and Jone weren't taking this rebound for granted. They had persuaded locals to cut back on fishing, enticed by the promise of well-paid resort jobs for the community, and had worked with the authorities to establish a coral nursery to replant nearby reefs. Divers were encouraged to visit the site and assist with the replanting. Was all the expense and effort worth it?

'Looking at all the locals whom we have trained to become divers… and the excitement of every local we take to the reef, we can strongly say it does,' Marina told me. 'And the guests turn into ocean ambassadors too.'

The second leg of our journey took us back to the beaten path on Viti Levu, the gateway to Fiji's infamous shark diving sites. Our guides (and guardians) for the cage-free dives were from Aqua Trek, with a spotless safety record and an all-local dive team armed with underwater shepherd's crooks to gently nudge sharks away if they got too close.

Plunging into Beqa Lagoon off the island's southern coast, dozens of reef, nurse, and lemon sharks circled around us, mere inches away. But the stars of the show were the bull sharks. Displaying none of the raw aggression they are famed for, the muscular figures largely ignored us, far more interested in the fish heads in the feeder and the schools of fish all around the reef.

The feeder filled with discarded tuna heads from a nearby processing plant is what has made the shark dives controversial: some argue that supplementary feeding could alter shark behaviour and disrupt local ecosystems. I will admit that part of me – the part with an academic background in conservation biology and a preference for leaving nature alone – was wary. But Jona, our affable dive guide, had a heartfelt take. 'Before we began the shark dives, I remember locals would hunt sharks to make a living. Now, we're able to show our community that they're worth protecting.' Studies have found that sharks are

Diving with sharks in Beqa Lagoon.

not permanently attracted to the area, and that supplementary feed only constitutes a small part of their diets.[10]

Uneasy as it may be for purists, the results have been striking. Over the years, the villages adjoining the lagoon relinquished their fishing rights in exchange for a levy paid back to the community and jobs with dive operators; in 2004, a marine protected area was declared, and later expanded to a thirty-mile 'shark corridor' along the coast. Fish populations have rebounded, with the main threat now coming from foreign fishing vessels.

Having survived my swim with the sharks in Beqa, I cast my mind back to a trip I had taken several years ago to Palau, another tourism-dependent Pacific Island nation endowed with natural treasures. Palau has a far smaller population – around 20,000 inhabitants – and has chosen a slightly different path. In 2009, Palau designated the world's first 'shark sanctuary', banning all commercial shark fishing in its waters. In 2020, it took a far bolder step, prohibiting all fishing and mining in 80 per cent of its waters, with the remaining 20 per cent reserved for local fishermen only. The result was an enormous marine protected area – the sixth largest in the world.

Palau's forward-looking government acted on a message that scientists had been sending for years: that commercial overfishing was, in a word, unsustainable. Indeed, fish populations have rebounded within protected areas and begun to spill over to the zones where fishing is allowed, just like the experts predicted.[11] But in Palau, as in Fiji, healthy reefs were the basis for a dive-tourism economy that drew visitors from all over the world – forming a small part of the $36 billion that reefs generate in tourism income globally.[12] On one dive at the Blue Corner site, I saw more sharks than I could count; at another, I saw schools of barracuda so large they blocked out the sun. In this wondrous, watery world, I felt as close to true wilderness as I had ever been.

To my mind, Viani Bay, Beqa and Palau offered three distinct, but distinctly pragmatic, examples that prove that nature can be worth more alive than dead. All were works in progress and had been rattled by a global pandemic. But inviting sustainable numbers of visitors in to experience these places seemed a great deal better for people and the planet than the unchecked destruction that is too often the default, to say nothing of the threats from overfishing and rising seas that can only be weathered if these places can create resilient local economies to pay for adaptation.

From birdwatching in Malaysia to gorilla hikes in Rwanda and caiman-spotting in Costa Rica, wild places across the world – on land and in the ocean – have leant on ecotourists to pay for preservation. I could write endlessly about the wonders of such places, and about the committed, thoughtful individuals who are paving the way for the ecotourism experiences of the future. Equally, however, it is clear to me that there are real questions and concerns around ecotourism that deserve our attention. The oldest business case for nature might also be the one that comes with the most baggage.

Critiques of ecotourism began in earnest in the early 2000s, as it became evident that the lofty ideals that had animated interest in the post-war era had given way to a messier reality.

The first question is a definitional one. What constitutes true ecotourism? Intuitively, ecotourism must involve treading lightly and providing benefits for nature and local people. Ideally, it might also induce mindset shifts in the visitors themselves, by leaving them with a stronger sense of the value of nature and the need to protect it. Various attempts have been made to define ecotourism, but the one in David Fennell's 2008 book, *Ecotourism*, offers what I find the most comprehensive, if tonally somewhat academic, take on the question.

> [Eco-tourism is a] sustainable, non-invasive form of nature-based tourism that focuses primarily on learning about nature first-hand, and which is ethically managed to be low impact, non-consumptive, and locally orient-ed.[...] It typically occurs in natural areas and should contribute to the conservation of such areas.[13]

In 2010, Ralf Buckley took it one step further and coined the term 'conservation tourism', which he defined as a subset of ecotourism 'that makes an ecologically significant net-positive contribution to the effective conservation of biological diversity'.[14] In this chapter, I use the umbrella term 'ecotourism', while recognising that the cases I highlight fit within Buckley's higher standard.

Either definition sounds wonderful. So perhaps the real question lies in who gets to claim the labels of ecotourism or conservation tourism, particularly in the absence of a global certification scheme that is universally trusted and widely used. It is possible to have tourism take place in wild areas that fails to meet the criteria laid out above; indeed, such instances are precisely the ones that have rightly led to howls of greenwashing. But, from my research and travels, there are myriad places where things are, in fact, being done the way they should. Still, some questions stood out to me when attempting to assess the broader impact of ecotourism.

Does responsible tourism of this sort actually benefit natural ecosystems? Some biologists have highlighted the impact that human visitors might have on animal behaviour. From gorillas that become accustomed to human trekkers, to the curious flightless birds that waddle up to visitors on the predator-free islands off Australia and New Zealand, it appears irrefutable that this is true in some places. But other studies have found that these impacts are overstated at the landscape scale. In any case, some have argued that the downsides, where present, are worth it. Buckley and his team, in a wide-ranging study of endangered species such as lions, tigers, wolves and rhinos, found that ecotourism had conservation benefits that outweighed the impacts and contributed to the survival of these rare animals.[15, 16]

What of the impact on local communities? The logic of ecotourism only really works if the people who rely on these natural wonders can share in the rewards. Here, the evidence is more mixed. In some places, like the sea turtle sanctuaries of Costa Rica and the wildlife reserves of Ecuador, researchers have established a positive link between ecotourism and community livelihoods. Zooming out, it's clear that tourism is vital economically for many countries and regions; beyond the direct impacts, the tax revenue generated from tourism indirectly funds a host of social infrastructure. But an intuitive sense that tourism revenue is valuable masks some thornier issues.

For one, the benefits might not flow to locals, particularly where the ecotourism label is misused as a front for extractive, unsustainable mass tourism. In some cases, like in Nepal, researchers found that these benefits, where directed to locals, were ultimately too small to prevent degradation.[17]

But there is also the question of the counterfactual – what would have happened in the absence of ecotourism? Would local communities in natural areas have remained small and ecologically benign, or would more extractive industries have taken over? This can be the hardest question to answer. Human stories – like the ones of the shark-fishermen-turned-guardians of Beqa – might offer some clues. But there is the more recent, and deeply disturbing, example of Venezuela's Amazon. Years of political turmoil in the country has killed off a once-thriving ecotourism industry; by 2022, even the deepest reaches of the Canaima national park were becoming disfigured by illegal mining. Reporting by the *Financial Times* and others told a tragic tale of tourism workers becoming wildcat miners in a desperate bid to make ends meet.[18]

Ultimately, ecotourism is a conscious choice on the part of visitors and hosts. But more and more places are choosing to do things sustainably, and attract tourists who spend a little more, stay a little longer, tread a little more lightly – even at the cost of numbers through the gate.

'We're no longer looking at pure volume coming in,' Brent Hill, chief executive of Tourism Fiji, told me, pointing to Fiji's renewed focus on attracting higher-value tourists and dispersing them across the archipelago's 330 islands. 'If people are really engaged with Fiji's environment, and they're doing things like planting coral or mangroves when they're here, they're going to protect it, come back, and spend a fair bit more as well.'

If places like Bali and Cancún in Mexico need a break from rampant overtourism, there are others that could use a little more attention. In Brazil, for instance, the Amazon is iconic, even if relatively few tourists actually visit it. But fewer still have even heard of the Pantanal, the world's largest tropical wetland. Located bang in the middle of South America, the Pantanal is home to the beady-eyed caiman, and the stealthy jaguars that hunt them. But the birds – from the stunning, cobalt-blue hyacinth macaw to the gigantic Jabiru stork, the largest flying bird in the Americas, and the equally tall, though flightless, emu-like rhea – take centre stage here. The Pantanal is both a unique biodiversity hotspot for its resident fauna and an important rest stop for migratory birds flying up and down the length of the Americas.

In the spring of 2022, I was fortunate to visit this watery wonder in the midst of its wettest season. Rains had inundated the land as far as the eye could see, giving the appearance of a sunken prairie, with grasses and water lilies interspersed by thickets of trees, and more shades of green than I had realised the human eye could perceive. This far off the beaten path, in low season, there wasn't a single (eco) tourist in sight other than me and the small group of friends I had enticed to join me.

Roberto Klabin is a Brazilian industrialist and conservationist who turned his childhood home in the Pantanal into the Caiman Ecological Refuge, kick-starting the region's still-nascent ecotourism industry. 'Brazil as a whole is totally overlooked as a tourist destination [...] and hardly anyone who comes to Brazil is willing to travel all the way inland to the Pantanal,' he told me, pointing out that in 2018 Brazil received about six million visitors, mostly from neighbouring countries; that is, less than a sixth of Thailand's tally that same year for a country fifteen times larger.

Roberto, now engaged in a campaign to give the Pantanal its own legal code, was keenly aware of the ecosystem's fragility. With over 90 per cent of the wetland in private hands, the Pantanal's traditional, low-impact ranching was being supplanted by intensive agriculture even as the climate became warmer and drier. 'To show landowners that the Pantanal is worth preserving, we need people to come see, and pay for, the beauty of this ecological wonder,' he said. 'And this includes families from the skyscrapers of São Paolo, who haven't seen the natural wealth of their own country!'

Our visit to the Pantanal had brought us to Araras Eco Lodge, run by an old friend of Roberto's who had set up one of a handful of eco-lodges in the region. Starting off camping on an old ranch – it seemed all ecotourism stories began with pitching tents in the wilderness – Andre and his wife had slowly built Araras into a small-scale, low-impact tourist operation. Supportive regional government policies and the decline of the local cattle industry (albeit in favour of defor-esting the Amazon) had led to a wildlife rebound. 'I arrived in 1967, and it took me eleven years to see a jaguar. Nowadays, we go out from Araras lodge in one of our boats, head down to the refuge, see jaguars and come back for dinner!'

'The most rewarding part of this journey has been all the people we've worked with and trained, many of whom now run other sustainable businesses and create livelihoods for their communities,' Andre told me. Carlos, our eagle-eyed guide, was the perfect illustration of the economic opportunities that ecotourism had brought to the wetland. Recounting stories from his youth, when he and his friends would hunt caiman, capybara and birds of all sorts, Carlos explained how he had become an ardent conservationist. 'A macaw living happily in a tree now has economic value to us Pantaneiros!' he told me, delighted that he had been able to leave behind the life of a hunter in favour of something kinder to the wildlife that chattered and screeched all around us.

I bring up the Pantanal not only to emphasise the benefits of ecotourism, when done well, but also to highlight the uneven nature of its bounty. Not every ecosystem needs to be saddled with tourists; some are certainly best left alone. But places like the Pantanal, which already have a legacy of private land ownership, roads and lodges, could certainly use a few more visitors. In creating a business case for the blue flash of a macaw overhead or the glint of a caiman's teeth in a flooded field, ecotourism might be just what we need to save this wondrous wetland from being lost to row after row of soy.

The Pantanal wetland in its wettest season.

No examination of ecotourism can be complete without considering the carbon question.

This chapter has been filled with stories from places that are likely a long and carbon-spewing flight away from where you are right now. In the midst of the climate crisis, can we really justify this sort of travel, whatever the incidental benefits?

In the era of flight-shaming a little nuance might be helpful. The truth is that developing countries like Fiji and Palau, or far-flung parts of larger countries like the Pantanal in Brazil, are at the coalface of rising seas and extreme weather events but have done virtually nothing to contribute to the climate crisis. If each country has a notional carbon budget – an amount it is allowed to emit on the pathway to net zero by 2050 or some such date – then it makes little sense to treat all countries equally. Flying transatlantic to New York for a weekend getaway should rightly be seen as unnecessary and wasteful. But we could argue that places like Fiji deserve a notional, additional carbon budget that they can use to justify bringing in sustainable numbers of visitors independent of their personal carbon footprints. While offsets are by no means a free pass, purchasing high-integrity carbon removals could be an appropriate way to mitigate some of the climate harm caused by flying. Taking fewer trips and staying longer could help too.

Further, the carbon maths might not be quite as skewed as we might first imagine. If the counterfactual to ecotourism is the chopping down of forests for timber and agriculture, it's possible that helping fund the protection of natural carbon sinks could help counterbalance some of those travel emissions, even if they're not enrolled in a formal carbon credit programme. I won't pretend there's a clear net-zero case for ecotourism – there likely isn't – but the carbon benefits of conservation can't be ignored entirely.

What we mustn't do is penalise these places for their isolation. Even as we encourage all countries to cut their emissions, those with the broadest shoulders (and the greatest historical carbon emissions) must step up. The developed countries that are most culpable can first do their part and pay their fair share to help fund adaptation in poorer countries. And we will need to work urgently to decarbonise aviation so that faraway places can remain connected to the rest of a net-zero world.

Of course, ecotourism doesn't have to involve far-flung corners of the world: it's perfectly possible to be a thoughtful, nature-loving traveller closer to home, and we should all be sure to explore such opportunities in national parks and rewilding projects in our own neighbourhoods and countries. But ecotourism is ultimately most valuable for people who lack alternatives; for places that are not fortunate enough to be able to afford stable, taxpayer-funded government protection.

What principles might help fulfil the promise that ecotourism continues to hold?

As with many of the other business cases we explore in this book, greater rigour in how we define things is a good first step. Nature-based tourism – where tourists interact with nature – is one thing. Ecotourism, or conservation tourism, which actively benefits nature and people in an equitable, nonconsumptive manner, is another thing entirely.

Applying the moniker too widely risks diluting the term, but it looks unlikely that governments will step in and regulate. In their absence, both operators and visitors must strive for transparency – reporting and researching impacts respectively to encourage a race to the top. Local and international industry bodies can do their part too: it is time for them to come together to create a transparent, Fairtrade-style certification scheme for the highest performers.

An important ingredient of strong performance is the participation of the local communities that must ultimately be served by ecotourism. Best of all is when local communities themselves run ecotourism operations. Where outsiders are involved, they can start by paying heed to local and indigenous voices, inviting them into decision-making and respecting their right to decline to open up to the outside world. Rather than being party – willingly or unwillingly – to the fetishisation of their cultures, as often happens when tourist operators come in from outside, it would be far better if these peoples could make informed decisions and retain their agency and dignity. Once money does start flowing in, it's important that locals can share in the bulk of the benefits and gain good jobs, as they did in the community of Viani Bay.

Ecotourism operators must also partner with scientists and policymakers to funnel resources towards the protection of nature. In some cases, this might be through the payment of levies or taxes that fund research, law enforcement and monitoring. Several operators I came across had employed in-house scientists to study local ecosystems to ensure their activities remained low impact. Even the simple provision of data – through the eyes and ears on the ground – could be of service to broader conservation efforts. In 2022, the team at Mandai Nature, a conservation non-profit based in Southeast Asia, laid out their vision for conservation tourism; what stood out to me was their call for operators to define and deliver specific, measurable conservation goals in the areas they help protect and to report on their progress over time.[19]

Responsible operators can also play an important educational role, applying scientific methods to awareness-raising and seeking to win hearts and minds. The Oceanic Society's Blue Habits programme is one such effort that applies principles from behavioural science and collaborates with Stanford's design school to explore and prototype educational techniques that actually work. The group found that whale watching tours that incorporated their principles created statistically significant increases in participants' "'sense of

ocean identity", "connection between environmental consequences and personal responsibility", and "willingness to
engage in plastic-reducing behaviours'".[20]

We also need to avoid the trap of having too much of a good
thing. Ecotourism would quickly enter unsustainable territory
if numbers aren't kept in check. Indeed, many examples of
greenwashing began as small-scale efforts, but expanded at a
breakneck pace until they were indistinguishable from their
mass-tourist counterparts; many sites in the Mediterranean
and the Caribbean appear to have followed this path.

I saw first-hand what untrammelled tourism looks like
when I lived in southern Bali a few years ago. Mass tourism
and poorly planned infrastructure had resulted in a catastrophic
plastic and waste problem that choked Bali's mangroves and
rivers. Tucked away behind the airport stood a smoking
mountain of rubbish, sections of which would slide into the
sea under the weight of seasonal downpours.

As far back as the early 1990s researchers were highlighting
the tendency of small-scale tourism to bleed into mass tourism.
Katrina Brandon, for instance, wrote a review in 1996 for the
World Bank that remains relevant for decision-makers to this
day.[21] Speaking to her nearly three decades on, she reflected
on a key finding that felt both pragmatic and actionable.

'One of the points I tried to make was that you might have
sacrificial areas with mass tourism as a way of funding a broader
park system. With a sound legal framework, communities in

natural areas can still get paid from mass tourism through a revenue-sharing mechanism. It seemed to me even back then that in a number of places, it would benefit communities in a fairer way than what I was seeing and better protect sensitive habitats.' Existing areas with mass tourism can still have a place in a country's development mix; areas that have already been built over and degraded can offer opportunities for large-scale, nature-based tourism if they can then generate revenue to protect more pristine places without burdening them with too many tourists.

Indeed, even long-suffering Bali still had stunning upland rice terraces, forests and a few reefs on the northern coast that were healthy. Tourism had lifted incomes across the island, and a new group of upwardly mobile environmentalists had begun to clamour for change. All hope was not lost, and perhaps even places like Bali will have second chances to chart a different path over time.

I remain convinced that we need a lighter-touch model for tourism, particularly in places that have thus far been spared the worst. Given the state of the planet's ecological collapse, governments need to show restraint, using science-based methods to determine sustainable numbers and employing permits and quotas where needed. They can take heart from the fact that this approach can often translate into higher value; ecotourism really isn't a numbers game. But visitors need to play their part too, viewing such trips as special rather than just another getaway, committing to staying longer in each place, and doing their part while they are there to leave nothing but footprints.

To see why this is ultimately worth it, I keep returning to the undeniable business logic of preserving nature – at least in certain places. In Palau, researchers identified one such business case: tourism contributes 31 per cent of the country's GDP, and a fifth of divers (like myself) chose Palau specifically to see the sharks. A back-of-the-envelope calculation, that excludes broader cultural and spiritual value, puts the value of the 100 sharks that inhabit its prime dive sites at $179,000 every year.[22] If they were all killed and sold for parts, the most they would fetch would be just over $10,000, one time. Studies of gorilla trekking in Rwanda and Uganda, and of game reserves in Southern Africa, have come to similar conclusions about how persuasive the case for ecotourism can be when the alternative is exploitation.

Back in 1996 Katrina Brandon's review found that '[despite] problems, ecotourism represents one of the few areas where the link between economic development and conservation of natural areas is potentially clear and direct'. While things have moved on since then, and new business cases have emerged – enough to fill a book, even – ecotourism's role in aligning economics and ecology remains relevant to this day.

But the very fact that ecotourism aligns economic incentives in such a money-minded manner has become a cause for criticism. 'Ecotourism can be regarded as part of the global capitalist system rather than any kind of challenge to it,' argues Professor Rosaleen Duffy, Chair of International Relations at Sheffield University and a specialist in the global politics of biodiversity conservation.[23] 'Ecotourism can neatly provide a source of agreement between organisations [like NGOs, multilateral organisations and governments] that would ordinarily be regarded as being in contestation with one another. [...] Such wide-ranging networks can then constitute powerful sets of supporters of ecotourism, which in turn serves to extend and intensify neoliberalism by capturing and entraining nature to the logics of global capital.'

Such concerns aren't entirely misplaced – after all, the presence of unlikely bedfellows should always give us pause. I wish there were tidier answers to these substantive questions. However, we do, for better or for worse, live in a global capitalist system, but one that we know can and should be reshaped to value natural and human capital in addition to financial capital. We don't have time to wait and wish for perfect outcomes. Instead, we do have a very human need to move, paired with a growing appreciation for what thoughtful ecotourism should look like. So, in the absence of large numbers of altruists willing to part with their money to 'visit' a place via video link, inviting smaller numbers of visitors to experience nature's glory first-hand remains an important way to create win–wins, however small, for people and the wonderful, wild planet we live in.

As engaging as wildlife documentaries and books might be, nothing comes close to the real thing. So, while even the most thoughtful ecotourists might not be blameless altruists, many do leave transformed by the experiences they have, bolstering the intrinsic case for nature that critics rightly emphasise. Those shifts in mindsets and attitudes can last a lifetime, making this grand old case for nature more relevant than ever in an age of distraction and digital dislocation.

Rewild and Regenerate

I was, as ever, running late. 'Meet us by the stork nests,' a voice crackled over the phone as the midday sun rose high in the sky; off we went, bouncing down the dirt track in a well-worn 4x4, on a mission to locate my guides and fellow travellers for the morning's safari.

As I caught my breath and offered my apologies, I took in the lush landscape. Thickets of trees were woven into a tapestry of grasslands and grassy glades, dotted with wildflowers, abuzz with bees. Free-roaming herbivores ambled around, picking at the greenery and paying little heed to their visitors. Overhead soared dozens of majestic white storks, circling ever higher as they rode that spring afternoon's thermals. Nature, seemingly untrammelled, all the way to the horizon and beyond.

But I wasn't in the plains of Serengeti or Yellowstone's high plateau. I was only sixteen miles from London's Gatwick

Airport, on Knepp Castle Estate in West Sussex. I had come to see a two-decade-long experiment in bringing nature back into the agricultural system. At Knepp, they had set out to 'rewild' this corner of the Sussex Weald; to revive it in both ecological and financial terms.

Knepp hadn't always offered this prelapsarian vision of a Britain before the ploughs took over. When Charlie Burrell inherited the estate from his grandfather at the age of twenty-two, it had been intensively farmed for decades. Initially hewing to orthodoxy, Charlie and his wife Isabella Tree began making large investments in machinery and modern breeding to try to turn the farm around. All to no avail: despite all the investment and farming subsidies, Knepp simply would not turn a profit.

What they hadn't accounted for was the heavy West Sussex clay on which Knepp Castle Estate stood. The intensive farming operation the family had tried to build over generations was simply unsuitable for the ecology of the region. Knepp racked up over £1.5 million in debt before Isabella and Charlie decided to try something different. With support from government schemes designed to pay for regeneration, the pair decided to turn their intensive agriculture operation into a nature restoration site, introducing Exmoor ponies, deer, longhorn cattle and Tamworth pigs and letting nature run riot on the 3,500-acre farm.

'That first year, I can remember walking outside, walking through wildflowers, hearing the insects and birds coming back, and realising it had all been worth it,' Isabella said as we returned to the castle for lunch. Isabella's bestselling book, *Wilding*, offers a vivid retelling of the Knepp story, and the trials and tribulations that they ultimately overcame to bring their vision to life.

The estate now hosts one of the largest and most diverse collections of animal life in the UK: nightingales, turtle doves, dozens of species of butterflies including the rare purple emperor, thirteen species of bats and all five native species of owl. In 2020, the first white storks to hatch in the country in over 600 years emerged from their shells in Knepp, following the reintroduction of a species long considered extinct as a breeding bird in Britain.[1] In 2021, two beavers had been introduced to the nearby River Adur, the first in the area in over four centuries.[2] Even the more common species were a delight to observe; sinking into lawn chairs on a wildflower lawn behind the castle, Isabella, Charlie and I watched as a herd of red deer frolicked around Knepp Mill Pond to a soundtrack of copious birdsong.

The result hasn't just been a heartwarming wildlife rebound; Knepp now turns a handsome profit, beating the per-hectare income of the average farm in lowland England – even those on better quality soil – with sales of its 'wild range' venison, pork and beef stacked on top of ecotourism revenue from visitors, rental of post-agricultural buildings for storage, light industrial use and office space, and environmental payments from the state.

* * *

Free-roaming Exmoor ponies graze at Knepp.

Knepp is no longer a farm, but is now held up as an example of 'rewilding', which can refer to everything from the reintroduction of wolves to Yellowstone National Park to the floodplain, peatland and woodland restoration that Cairngorms Connect is embarking on in Scotland. It goes without saying that in highly degraded ecological systems, like those in the UK and much of Europe, rewilding may look rather tame: no large carnivores are likely to stalk London's periphery any time soon.

'What we learnt over time was that the primary purpose for Knepp was restoration. It's creating new habitats for the future, and a life raft for nature. Secondary to that is the production of food,' Charlie told me, emphasising Knepp's role as distinct from, but complementary to, the agricultural system. 'To create that broader support system to make healthy food, we need to restore soils – we've got to restore our landscapes.

'So you need these core areas, which are for nature, that are maybe 30 per cent of our land; the other 70 per cent is going to have to be more productive, and productive in a way that is regenerative,' Charlie told me, showing me an artist's impression he had commissioned to bring that vision of the English countryside to life. The existing landscape of mono-cropped barley, intersected by two highways and a hemmed-in canal, had been reimagined: wildflower meadows and wilder rivers had taken over, the soils and skies teeming with life.

'So core areas are rewilded, but you also have a land-scape that becomes full of corridors and opportunities for movement [for wildlife]. With regenerative agriculture and rewilding working together, you end up with a very different landscape, a very different future, which is productive, as well as being incredibly good for nature.' Charlie was now working with neighbouring farmers to bring this vision to life through Weald-to-Waves, a project seeking to connect Knepp to the Sussex coast.

Not all places need to become like Knepp; but rewilding projects like Knepp, and existing wildernesses, need to be part of a regenerating rural tapestry that includes highly productive, low-impact agricultural production, complemented by novel food technologies and largely plant-based diets that can help us demand less from our land. Setting aside more areas for rewilding, particularly when land is degraded or unproductive, is only part of the answer; we will also need to bring life back to the actively managed agricultural areas that feed the world. Restoring nature in and around our working lands doesn't only offer a path forward for a food system that is running out of juice, it comes with a compelling economic case to boot.

What does it mean to engage in nature-positive food production? As is too often the case across the sectors we cover in this book, there is no commonly agreed, comprehensive definition of regenerative agriculture. What producers have instead is a toolkit of nature-friendly interventions that they can apply to meet the unique characteristics of their land.

Soil health is central to regenerative agriculture, and one way to encourage the earth beneath farms to teem with life is to leave it alone. Conventional farming involves the tilling of soil between harvests – often with heavy machinery – to remove weeds and break up the soil for new planting. But tilling is, in short, terrible for the soil, making it easier for wind and water to blow away the precious organic matter that sustains plant life. Regenerative practices forego tillage in favour of planting 'cover crops' such as rye and clover between harvests, to keep nutrients and life locked in the ground.

Regenerative agriculture also involves minimising, and in some cases eliminating, chemical inputs. Synthetic fertilisers, pesticides and herbicides are the backbone of modern farming; the dramatic rise in crop production globally has been made possible by their widespread use beginning in the second half of the twentieth century. But we now know that these synthetic additives have catastrophic effects on our wildlife and waterways, and perhaps even our health. Instead, regenerative farms try to do the same with diverse natural systems. Animal droppings can do the job of synthetic nitrogen or phosphorus; herbivores, insects and birds can keep pests and weeds in check.

Another core tenet of regenerative practices is an embrace of ecological diversity. Regenerative producers shun the mono-cultures that have long been favoured in Europe or the American Midwest. Instead, they seek to create diverse collections of plants and animals – some wild, others domesticated

– that can feed off each other and create a beneficial ecosystem on each farm. Trees are increasingly recognised as an important part of the equation: agroforestry and silvopasture are both terms used to refer to the integration of trees into productive croplands or grazing systems, providing myriad benefits including shade, soil protection, carbon storage and supplementary income from tree crops themselves. Replanting hedgerows, which were ripped out in favour of monocultures, can help boost biodiversity by providing shelter and forage for beneficial species. On-farm diversity doesn't only consist of the life forms we can see: bacteria, a billion of which can be held in a single teaspoon of healthy soil, play an essential role in breaking down organic matter and returning nutrients to the roots of crops. Healthier soils typically have larger and more diverse sets of these invisible allies.

Domesticated animals often, though by no means always, play a part in regenerative systems. This is particularly true of places with poor soils that historically would have been mixed woodland or open prairie, like Knepp, where original grazers and their predators have long gone extinct. Even row-crop systems growing wheat or maize can bring in domesticated animals – think chickens or ducks – to run free across fields, eating pests and weeds and cycling nutrients through their droppings.

How is rewilding different from regenerative agriculture? It can help to think of them both as forms of landscape regeneration, leaning on the same principles of restoring biological diversity, but ultimately with different aims. In rewilding projects, nature protection and restoration is the goal, and food is a relatively minor by-product. These places often charge a premium for their products and can often receive the majority of their income from other sources like ecotourism or ecosystem service payments.

For regenerative agriculture the primary goal is nature-friendly food production; here, regenerative principles can be put to work to transform more traditional, and traditionally productive, farming landscapes and produce far more substantial quantities of food. Steps to adopt no-till or cover cropping can have big benefits for nature and farmers' bottom lines. A Soil Health Institute review of 100 American row-crop farmers across nine states who had taken up these practices found that 85 per cent of them experienced a boost to their incomes.[3] Some of that came in the form of lower costs on inputs like labour and fertiliser and higher prices on outputs, but two-thirds actually experienced increased yields. Beyond the direct benefits, nearly all noted that soil health, water quality and crop resilience had improved noticeably.

At the very least, nature-positive interventions can help cushion impacts on nature even in more intensive agricultural systems. In California's Central Valley, for instance, bio-based inputs – such as nitrogen-fixing microbes sprayed or drip-fed to plants – are being pioneered by companies like Pivot Bio and MyLand to replace synthetic fertilisers and increase yields. Meanwhile, in north India's agricultural belt, the Happy Seeder – a tractor-mounted machine that allows farmers to sow seeds without turning over the soil – helps them to adopt no-till, no-burn practices that lock carbon in the soil and cut the rice-stubble smoke that envelops Delhi every winter.

While I refer to the different shades of regenerative food production described above as 'nature-positive', not everyone will agree that farmers at the mechanised, automated end of the spectrum should qualify for the 'regenerative' moniker. Fully organic, chemical-free production may well be suitable for some crops and preferred by some discerning consumers; we should absolutely encourage those markets and methods to scale. But, to my mind, not all regeneration needs to be organic and to eliminate entirely the use of chemical inputs in order to bring life back to the land.

Nature-positive agriculture for the majority of the farming system is ultimately about finding an equilibrium point that lies well short of the chemical-intensive, soil-depleting monocultures that are currently the norm. Not every parcel of land can become as wild and inspiring as Knepp; we're only just embarking on a worldwide journey to restore nature to our agricultural lands, and even baby steps to move away from the industrial agricultural default surely deserve to be cheered on.

* * *

Any discussion of regenerative agriculture returns to a fundamental question: without intensive farming practices, can we grow enough food to feed the world?

While I firmly believe in the need to shift away from industrial agriculture, those of us who hope to chart a different course must first admit that the old model has resulted in tremendous, if unsustainable, leaps in productivity and prevented widespread hunger. While Paul Ehrlich's warnings in the 1970s of a 'population bomb' and global famine never came to pass, it is easy to see why such predictions were made: in 1966, the US sent a quarter of its wheat output to India to avert famine, and it wasn't clear at all that the Malthusian paradigm could be broken.

Then came the work of scientists like Norman Borlaug, a central figure in the 'Green Revolution' that selectively bred hardier and higher-yielding crops and spread them across both the developed and developing world. He received a Nobel Peace Prize in 1970 for his work in averting mass hunger and raising farmer incomes. Today, places like Punjab in India boast some of the highest per-acre yields in the world. Borlaug's work was later followed by a raft of genetically modified organisms – using technology to do what he had done through manual hybridisations – that boosted yields in the places that allowed GMOs, like the US, to unheard-of levels.

But all of this came at a tremendous ecological cost. Monocultures of crops like wheat, rice, oil palm and barley, along with industrial beef and dairy production (which also rely on cereal and soy crops for supplementary feed), have led to the conversion of 40 per cent of the Earth's surface into croplands and pastures. Agriculture is the dominant driver of deforestation in places like the Amazon and Borneo. On top of its ever-expanding footprint, modern farming is thirsty; over 70 per cent of our freshwater use is devoted to agriculture, much of it now through irrigation rather than rain-fed.

Most dramatic of all has been the increase in chemical inputs. Since 1961, global consumption of nitrogen fertiliser has grown ninefold, while potassium and phosphorus use have each grown about fourfold. The rise of monocultures has also removed the biological controls that naturally keep pests and diseases in check, meaning farmers have to compensate artificially. Over four million tonnes of chemical pesticides are now slathered onto farms, killing off any glimmer of ecological balance and making these systems entirely dependent on the heavy hand of human management. These inputs then spill over into the wider ecosystem, creating dead zones in water bodies and contributing directly to climate change and air pollution in the form of nitrous oxide and ammonia emissions.

As on-farm biodiversity has collapsed, so too have the carbon stocks that these soils, and standing forests that have been cleared for growing or grazing, once held. At least a third of the world's soils are in 'poor or very poor' condition, according to the Food and Agriculture Organisation of the United Nations (FAO) in 2015.[4] An estimated 133 billion tonnes of carbon has been released from soils since humans began farming 12,000 years ago, with most of that loss taking place in the last 200 years.[5]

Rather than asking whether we can afford, in food security terms, to adopt regenerative agriculture, the better and more urgent question is whether we can afford to go on as we are. While yields from conventional agriculture might seem sky-high right now, to me and many others, our food system looks like a house built on a rapidly crumbling ecological foundation. As well as it may have served us up to this point, the rising tide of pests, plant diseases, soil erosion, pollution and climate change look set to send yields backwards in the coming decades.

One approach to keep the current system ticking over would be to convert wild land to cropland and pasture to replace degraded landscapes. Indeed, this is the solution that the beef ranchers of Brazil and the crop-farmers of Canada and Russia are choosing – swapping lifeless soils that they helped kill off for rich, loamy forest and taiga soils that can give them a few more good years. But as we will see elsewhere in this book – and, indeed, as common sense dictates – this path offers no way out of the mess we find ourselves in; it only pushes back the day of reckoning, and only at the cost of continued biodiversity collapse and carbon release. A better way is surely possible.

Rather than endlessly looking further afield for new places to farm, nature-positive practices can help bring back vitality to the same working lands we currently occupy – and perhaps even shrink the footprint of agriculture in the years to come.

One line of evidence comes from the Rodale Institute, a nonprofit dedicated to research into organic farming. Side-by-side field trials over thirty years have shown that while yields tend to decline slightly for the first year or two as farms transition to regenerative practices, yields can then jump up to levels similar to conventional farming. The real benefit, though, comes when farms are stressed by drought or pestilence; the diversity inherent to regenerative agriculture can make farms more resilient. As I mentioned earlier, farms don't have to cut out inputs entirely; the targeted application of herbicide, for instance, can help keep yields high in regenerative systems that come under assault from weeds in the early years. Finally, a whole suite of new studies have shown how microbial diversity can play an important, and grossly underappreciated, role in long-term soil and plant health – diversity that can be meaningfully enhanced through regenerative practices and bio-based alternatives to fertilisers and pesticides.

Real-world cases show how output can be maintained, or even boosted, including in large-scale regenerative systems. The Balbo Group in Brazil adopted soil-friendly machinery, biological pest control and organic fertilisers across its entire operations, resulting in a 20 per cent jump in productivity after an initial transition period.[6] Balbo's organic sugar brand, Native, produces 75,000 tonnes of the stuff a year: more than a third of the world's market for organic sugar.

Feeding the world this way has even won backing from Norman Borlaug's International Maize and Wheat Improvement Centre (CIMMYT), the same organisation that oversaw the global takeover of high-yielding, famine-fighting monocultures. The organisation now backs an approach it calls 'sustainable intensification', which incorporates many of the same nature-positive principles we've explored here.

'The Green Revolution had unintended environmental and social consequences,' the organisation acknowledged in 2018, saying its scientists have begun 'placing stronger emphasis on environmental and social aspects – such as conserving soil and water, and ensuring social inclusion of marginalised groups'.[7] Today, CIMMYT has pivoted to researching conservation agriculture; its SIMLESA project, which ran from 2014 to 2018, showed, for instance, that sustainable intensification led to a 60–90 per cent increase in water infiltration and a 10–50 per cent increase in maize yields in Malawi. In Ethiopia, crop incomes nearly doubled with crop diversification, reduced tillage and improved varieties.[8]

I personally remain doubtful that regenerative and organic farming can consistently match the yields of the most productive industrial systems. Indeed, a comprehensive report by the Food and Land Use Coalition examining over fifty other published papers on a range of regenerative methods, from no-till to agroforestry, concluded that the positive impacts on soil carbon and biodiversity were clear. However, they found that the yield impacts varied depending on the system and the baseline they were starting from. 'The good news is that there are many regenerative agricultural systems that are profitable, sequester carbon and enhance biodiversity,' they concluded.[9]

We don't have to prove that regenerative agriculture produces better yields in every single case, though; it's fine to admit that conventional agriculture on rich, unspoilt soils may well yield better results for quite a while. But little of the world has such soils left to plant crops on. Where we are today is not where we were at the advent of the Green Revolution. Times and soils have changed, and we need to change with them.

The question of yields is inextricably tied to the ultimate purpose of all that production: to sustain our diets.

Those diets have steadily gotten more meat-heavy over the years: global meat production has increased more than fivefold since 1961, even as the world population has only just over doubled.[10] This trend has closely tracked rising incomes, with residents of rich countries eating far more meat than those in less well-off ones.

Beyond the moral unease that comes with raising billions of animals in cramped conditions and slaughtering them en masse – Henry Mance's book *How to Love Animals* offers a clear-eyed and non-judgemental look into this topic – lies the sheer ecological cost of meat production. Only about 55 per cent of the calories that crops produced globally are used to feed humans directly, while over a third is diverted to feed animals.[11] Animals are incredibly inefficient middlemen in the food pyramid: only around a tenth of the calories fed to animals are then in turn made available as meat and dairy for human consumption. Our diets are also accompanied by ludicrous amounts of food waste; about 17 per cent of all the food we produce is discarded, adding up to nearly a billion tonnes of food that could have filled our stomachs.[12]

The reality is that we already produce more than enough calories to feed nine billion people a healthy, balanced, mostly plant-based diet. And for much of history, this was exactly the sort of diet that prevailed across the world; the dramatic rise in meat consumption in the last half-century or so is a historical anomaly. One proposal for rebalancing our diets comes from the EAT-Lancet commission, which constructed a 'planetary health diet' that didn't cut out meat and dairy entirely but stripped them back to levels that are better for both people and the planet. A study in *Nature* found that adopting this diet across high income countries would free up an area slightly larger than the European Union and cut the carbon cost of the average diet by nearly two-thirds.[13]

Technology could be a powerful complement to nature-positive agriculture. Plant-based products like Impossible Burgers and Beyond Meat, as well as a growing pipeline of products based on precision fermentation or cellular cultivation, are creating impressive alternatives to animal protein. We might soon (and in the eyes of many, already do) live in a world where these products are close enough to their animal-derived counterparts. These tech-enabled alternatives also have far lighter ecological footprints: Impossible, for instance, claims that its burgers require 96 per cent less land and 87 per cent less water to produce compared to beef.[14] The upshot is that we could do something else with the vast areas we currently turn over to feeding herbivores. In his book *Regenesis*, environmental thinker George Monbiot convincingly argues that the key issue with animal agriculture is that it takes up so much space, both directly and to grow feed, that little is left for rewilding. He argues that 'farmfree' food made from new technologies like precision fermentation, paired with appropriate safeguards to ensure these innovations are treated as public goods, could be a key pathway out of our dependence on animal agriculture. Such technologies, if scaled up, could play an important role in taking the pressure off land.

But proponents of animal agriculture sometimes argue that there are marginal lands that are unsuitable for traditional agriculture, that there is effectively no agriculturally productive version of 'something else' for these lands. That may indeed be the case, but there are *ecologically* productive alternatives to intensive grazing, a system that ensures that once-diverse landscapes remain denuded and treeless. Changing that system will likely require us to confront our deep-rooted pastoralist fantasies that paint endless rolling hills of grass as essentially beautiful and natural, rather than the ecological deserts they often are.

Rather than vilifying farmers who intensively raise animals in order to satiate our meat addiction, we could demand less of these landscapes and compensate farmers fairly for providing ecological services instead. Imagine a world in which there are more Knepps: where we retreat from these 'marginal' lands and leave them to regrow as natural green spaces and wildlife habitats, while perhaps producing small quantities of quality meat from animals that have lived largely free-ranging lives.

I'm more than content with my own meat-free diet, a diet made easy and varied by the profusion of delicious plant-based proteins and meat-alternatives. Over time, though, I've come to appreciate just how much emotional and cultural value many of my friends attach to meat and dairy. I must concede that, despite better technology, smarter public policy and growing environmental awareness, it doesn't look as if meat will disappear entirely from our diets any time soon. Nor does it need to. All we need to do is turn meat back into a treat rather than a daily 'necessity' so that we can make space for nature by pausing, and then gradually reversing, our planet-wide agricultural sprawl.

Even if it's possible to feed the world and restore it at the same time, can farmers afford to make this change and still make a living? Is there really a business case for nature-positive agriculture or rewilding, even if it's the right thing to do?

'Charlie and I were not wilful destroyers. We simply had no incentive to think about nature,' Isabella Tree writes in *Wilding*. 'Like most farmers we considered ourselves stewards of the land while, deep down, we felt that nature was not a farming business. Nature was something that happened elsewhere, away from the hard-nosed economics of agriculture. We travelled the world to see wildlife. We campaigned to stop the felling of rainforests and the building of dams. Yet we were blind to what we were doing in our own back yard. Had intensive farming been profitable for us we would undoubtedly be doing it still.'[15]

Here's the thing: in a great many cases, intensive farming is only profitable because of the colossal subsidies that prop up the current system. In 2021, the UN estimated that governments give farmers $540 billion in subsidies annually, about 15 per cent of total agricultural production value. Over 90 per cent of that figure goes to subsidising 'harmful' – read conventional – intensive production methods.

Despite these subsidies, it surprised me to learn that Charlie and Isabella's previous financial woes were far from unique; most intensive farmers simply don't make very much money. In the US, over half of farms lose money in any given year.[16] In India, the fertiliser subsidies and minimum support prices that enabled the Green Revolution have still left many farmers eking out a precarious existence. Many rack up debts to buy seeds and chemicals before each harvest, with degraded soils and weather-related crop failures piling on the pressure. Their stories often end in tragedy; over 10,000 Indian farmers take their own lives annually.[17] The picture is similar across the developed and developing world. While large agricultural producers and processors make tidy profits, the business case for intensive agriculture is far weaker for ordinary taxpayers and smallholders.

Take a step back, and it becomes clear that intensive methods can only produce cheap and plentiful food by depleting the stocks of soil health and biodiversity that sustain production. At some point, it follows that these stocks can no longer sustain the low-cost, high-productivity farming that we have come to take for granted. Regeneration, then, is ultimately the act of rebuilding those stocks to arrive at a system that is sustainable over the long term.

Russ Conser, who works with dozens of nature-positive ranchers in the US to help sell their regenerative products directly to consumers, helped me understand the recent surge of interest in regenerative agriculture among producers. 'It's being driven not by an influx of capital or investment. It's being driven by farmers looking for a better way because they're fed up with industrial agriculture,' he said, 'whether they're sick of the high cost of seed and fertiliser, or the unfair industry architecture that means prices are going up for consumers and profits are going up for Big Beef. Farmers are not seeing any of that value because suppliers don't have any power under the current market [structure].'

Charlie Burrell pointed to other farmers in his network who had engaged in more productive regenerative agriculture – rather than rewilding as at Knepp – and turned their finances round as well. 'Once you've got rid of the plough, you've got rid of the need to house a huge quantity of machinery and equipment, so you've freed up a whole load of capital and space to do other things and find other income streams,' he said. 'You've got a system that's no longer so hungry on fuel and energy and big machines. With regenerative agriculture, you add nature back into the landscape, [and] you've suddenly got a system that's really singing, that also happens to be financially brilliant for them.'

Halfway across the world, Charles Massy cut costs by as much as 90 per cent at his sheep station in western Australia after transitioning to nature-positive methods in 2000.[18] In his book *Call of the Reed Warbler*, Massy, now a passionate advocate for regenerative agriculture down under, writes about how this transition helped create a more profitable operation while simultaneously restoring habitats for wildlife – like the eponymous warbler – in a previously desertified, overgrazed landscape.[19]

Regeneration can be particularly cost-effective on land that has already been degraded, and therefore become unsuitable for industrial farming. Some estimates, such as one from SLM Partners, a regenerative agriculture investor, suggest that as much as one third of the world's land could fit this description after decades of draining soils. SLM calls their strategy of investing in degraded landscapes, which can typically be bought or leased at throwaway prices, 'ecological turnaround'.[20] The firm has bought degraded pastureland in Chile and Australia with a goal of doubling production through regenerative methods. Similar techniques are being applied in the degraded pasturelands of Brazil and the previously deforested soils of Indonesia and Malaysia.

Beyond cutting land and input costs, growers and ranchers transitioning to nature-positive methods often find that their higher-quality products fetch premium prices. Knepp's wildland meat and Blue Nest's beef both sell for more than their bog-standard counterparts; the same can be true for shade-grown coffee, cocoa and vanilla. As more and more producers transition to regenerative methods, these premiums may well disappear over time. Still, in the short term, they can provide a helpful leg up for early adopters able to tell a compelling story about their products.

Carbon markets are beginning to offer an additional revenue stream for farmers willing to make these shifts. In the US, for instance, farmer cooperative Land O'Lakes has teamed up with Microsoft to reward farmers for shifting to practices that support carbon storage in their soils. The Truterra Carbon programme launched in 2021 and pays farmers about $20 for every tonne of *additional* carbon they store; to put that in perspective, a regenerative farm can store between 0.2 and 0.75 tonnes annually on each acre.[21] In the UK, France and Belgium, Soil Capital has launched a similar scheme that pays out at least £23 for every tonne of carbon locked away.[22]

Some caution may be wise here. The science of soil carbon is far less advanced, and settled, than its tree carbon counterpart. For one, soil carbon estimates can vary dramatically from field to field, and between deeper and shallower soil layers, even when measured in a lab, let alone using remote methods.

To add to the complexity, the carbon storage benefits of regenerative practices are still being worked out, and different studies have thrown up a range of results. Take no-till, where the carbon impact appears to vary based on the environment. 'In some contexts – colder, wetter climates, for instance – increased carbon at the surface and reduced carbon at depth tend to offset each other. In warmer and drier environments, reduced carbon storage at depth seems to be less common and the overall effect of no-till on carbon storage may be positive,' writes CarbonPlan in a review of the literature.[23] Finally, the risk of all that carbon being released back into the air if a field is later ploughed and turned back into a conventional set-up is also real – although farmers on these programmes typically make a ten-year commitment to maintain their practices. To be clear, agroforestry systems that integrate *trees* into crop- or pastureland are not subject to the same degree of uncertainty, and carbon projects that incentivise agroforestry adoption are growing in their number and sophistication. That is welcome news.

On *soil* carbon, scientists and business models are getting smarter, and there are certainly buyers happy to tolerate some uncertainty in the interim to help kickstart this market. Farmers willing to be early adopters in this burgeoning soil carbon market might find that carbon can add another layer to the increasingly favourable economics of nature-positive production. Still, I see the soil carbon benefits of regenerative agriculture as a potential sweetener to the very real benefits that it can have for nature; the benefits that should, by themselves, create a powerful case for change.

While the long-term economic picture might look rosy, producers are often put off by the transition costs in the early years when they must make new investments, change equipment, learn new skills and potentially accept lower yields for a year or two as a new ecology beds in. Farmers can't be expected to finance the transition to regeneration all by themselves, so large companies are beginning to step in. The

€25 billion food-products multinational Danone, for instance, is offering farmers long-term contracts to help them make investments into regenerative practices; in Europe, over 40 per cent of Danone's suppliers benefit from such contracts.[24] Equally, government grants and tax breaks are being recast to help farmers cross the financial chasm to a more profitable regenerative model, as we will see later in this chapter.

Transitions can be tricky and demand preparation. Sri Lanka's failed nationwide experiment with organic farming serves as a cautionary tale. In mid-2021, faced with a looming economic crisis and a shortage of hard currency, Sri Lanka's government imposed a complete ban on imports of synthetic fertilisers and pesticides, allegedly to save scarce dollars. But with virtually no transition time or support in the form of organic pesticides and fertilisers, the foolhardy policy went about as badly as one might expect; rice production dropped 20 per cent, deepening an economic crisis that in 2022 led the government to reverse course before it was toppled by popular protests. Few who understand nature-positive agriculture would recommend going about it the way the Sri Lankan government did, dealing a hammer blow to a food system that could, over several years, have been weaned off its dependence on chemical inputs. As strong as the long-term business case might be, Sri Lanka's experience should warn others of the dangers of shortcuts and wishful thinking over thoughtful planning and sound science.

In short, regenerative agriculture is no panacea. It won't, by itself, set farmers free from the current system or automatically transform their fortunes or those of our planet. But restoring soil health and ecosystem function is an investment in the future of our food security – an investment that we can't afford to delay and that can, over time, generate meaningful returns for rural economies.

As we've seen with other business cases, agreeing on common language could be a sensible step to bring clarity to the market. The US Department of Agriculture's USDA Organic certification scheme shows the effect a clear standard can have. First implemented in 2001, the label is now well-understood by producers and consumers alike, and has helped create a burgeoning market for organic produce.

Regenerative agriculture is a little trickier to pin down. A 2020 study of over 250 journal articles and websites found a vast array of definitions that were based on processes (such as cover crops, the integration of livestock, and reducing tillage), outcomes (improved soil health, sequestered carbon, and increased biodiversity, for example), or combinations of the two.[25]

Faced with a nascent and fragmented market, the paper's authors recommend the use of standards that will allow consumers to scrutinise claims. The Regenerative Organic Alliance, for instance, offers one standard. It builds on the

USDA Organic certification as a baseline, counting such work 'as part of the journey to Regenerative Organic Certification'. But the standards really prescribe processes, not outcomes, even as they aim for broadly better soil health and animal welfare.

Regardless of the standards we coalesce around, consumer awareness is key. 'There's this really troubling problem of the well-intentioned, partially educated consumer, who can surprisingly be a little bit more easily manipulated,' Russ Conser told me as he described his journey to setting up Blue Nest. 'The sector was just chock full of people that told a great story and were allowed to show you a picture of a cowboy on horseback wrangling horses, when in reality, that animal that's on your plate just came from the feedlot. The big question, at the end of the day, is: how fast can we grow an authentically informed and engaged consumer market coupled with an authentic supply chain?' Still, he remained optimistic that the impacts of regeneration would reveal themselves over time. 'Let nature itself be the judge,' he said. 'I think you'll know that those farms are working because when you walk into them, they're going to be lush with life, butterflies, bees, insects, birds, things that are very visible. And so it really won't matter whether they're large or they're small.'

But the question of whether farms are large or small is an important one to consider. Proponents of nature-friendly farming can't pay attention only to the big beasts of the agricultural economy. For all the tremendous impacts of large industrial farms, over 90 per cent of the 570 million farms on Earth are run by individuals and their families. They produce 80 per cent of the world's food, so bringing them on board with regenerative practices will be vital to the transition.[26]

After years of much talk and little action on nature-positive agriculture and rewilding, I was heartened to find initiatives popping up across sectors to help accelerate this long-overdue transition.

On one hand are non-profits like Mad Agriculture, a Boulder, Colorado–based organisation that is working to educate producers, finance transitions and market their regenerative products. 'The world that we are striving to create is so vastly different than the world that is, that nearly everything that we do bears certain madness,' the organisation says, justifying its name and highlighting the boldness of its vision. More such initiatives are needed; universities and social sector organisations played an important part in the Green Revolution, and the time has again come for them to help the world change course.

Private companies and investors are also getting into the business of landscape regeneration. Some, like Propagate Ventures, are providing analytics and insights to help land-owners integrate trees into pastureland. Others, like Nattergal in the UK, are attempting to replicate the Knepp model across

Europe by buying up and transforming degraded land with a view to proving the long-term profitability of rewilding projects.

But perhaps more important are governments and the reshaping of their agricultural subsidy schemes. From the American farming tax credits and the European Union's Common Agricultural Policy to fertiliser subsidies in places like India and Indonesia, governments too often entrench the system that has turned working land into ecological desert. But national administrations are inching towards rethinking the paradigm, despite lobbying from the players who profit off the current system.

In the UK, the government has embarked on a multi-year project to refashion agriculture subsidies to support nature and use 'public money for public goods'. The new Environmental Land Management (ELM) scheme, as it is called, was designed to replace the direct payments that the EU used to provide simply for farming land, with a set of incentives that pay for environmental outcomes.

Defra, the department in charge of ELMs, set out three new schemes at the start of 2023 after years of consultation. The first is a sustainable farming incentive for practices that improve soil health, for instance, which will be rewarded with as much as £58 per hectare – about the same as the average annual profit per hectare from conventional farming in the UK. The other two schemes relate to nature recovery (often used interchangeably with rewilding) at local and landscape scales, offering as much as £537 a hectare for restoring carbon-rich fenland.

'Given the market does not adequately reward the delivery of environmental public goods, ELM will be an effective way for the government to intervene and utilise public funding to deliver them,' states Defra, the department in charge of ELM. In a public consultation. The proof will be in the pudding as the scheme is incre- mentally rolled out in the coming years – assuming it is not scuppered or delayed by political uncertainty within the UK. Still, ELM offers a once-in-a-generation chance to reimagine the role of government in supporting nature in the UK and the hope is that models like these, whatever form they take, will further strengthen the business case for regeneration.[27]

Driving back to London from Knepp, I couldn't help but look differently at the fields I was whizzing past. What had in my mind been a green and pleasant land now stood in stark, still, homogeneous contrast to the diversity and vitality I had left behind. If regeneration was possible on a landscape as trimmed and manicured as Britain's, it surely could be adopted virtually anywhere, by any farmer, choosing any point on the spectrum that makes sense for their business and for the ecosystem they can help sustain.

But that day, economic logic had been complemented by something else: the sense of wonder that comes with a glimpse of what a wilder, more exciting agricultural hinterland could look like.

'I think that's what people find so inspiring… they look out at the view we have now and realise that this was all wheat fields in 2004,' Isabella told me as the red deer moved on, and our collective attention turned to the biscuit tin. 'Nature will bounce back if you do it the right way. In this age of eco-anxiety, the crisis we're facing can be very frightening. It renders you completely impotent. I've seen it in people's eyes… that sense of agency that they suddenly feel again when visiting places like Knepp.'

How right she was. Rewilding, regenerative agriculture, feeding the world without costing the Earth. Somehow, against the odds, it all felt within reach.

Urban Jungles

Singapore today is a byword for modernity. Two years after it gained independence from Britain in 1963, Malaysia expelled the city-state from its federation following race riots. Few expected what came next. Singapore embraced a trade-and-investment-led formula that turned it into the futuristic, cosmopolitan city-state we now know. Standing at the crossroads of Southeast Asia, it has one of the world's wealthiest and best-educated populations. Policy wonks across the political spectrum now point to this 'Asian Tiger' economy as a model for development.

But it wasn't that long ago that Singapore had actual tigers. The island lies at the southern tip of the Malay Peninsula in the heart of one of the most biodiverse ecoregions on the planet, a stone's throw from the jungles of Sumatra. 'There are always a few tigers roaming about Singapore, and they kill on average a Chinaman every day,' the storied British naturalist Alfred Russel Wallace wrote in 1854, speaking to the richness of the ecosystem even as he used language that would not pass muster today. Wallace used the then-ramshackle trading outpost as a base to explore the Malay Archipelago, coming up with the theory of evolution independently of Darwin and, in the eyes of many, being unfairly denied credit for the gruelling field work and scientific curiosity that had produced the insight.

Fast forward a century and a half, and it was clear why many from Europe and America felt this tiny island nation had left them in the dust, even if its developmental leap had come at the cost of certain freedoms. Landing in stunning, high-ceilinged Changi felt more like walking into an art gallery than an airport. A hyper-efficient transit system whisked me around the city in minutes on my bi-weekly visits from neighbouring Indonesia. Gleaming skyscrapers dotted the various quays that make up the city centre, each uniquely designed and instantly recognisable. The roads were remarkably free of congestion – the product of a surge-pricing system of tolls and severely restricted car ownership – in a refreshing contrast to traffic jams of Jakarta and Bali, where I was living. Singapore's three main constituent cultures – Chinese, Malay and Indian – had combined with the lingering imprint of British colonialism and the trappings of Western-style capitalism to produce a city that felt like it treasured the past even as it bounded into the future.

Despite all its technological sophistication, Singapore remains a prisoner of geography. Sitting just below the equator, the city-state is, in short, hot and wet. Temperatures regularly top 30°C year-round and, unlike in other parts of Asia, rain is a constant, rather than seasonal, feature of Singaporean life. When I was in Singapore, thunderstorms would loose themselves from overcast skies with little warning, sending smartly dressed office workers in the city's downtown scattering for shelter. Soon after, the sun would break through, puddles and glass towers would shimmer, and the humid heat would once again envelop everyone and everything in sight.

These challenges are only set to intensify as the planet warms. The Centre for Climate Research Singapore has projected that if we keep going down the path we are on, the city-state will be up to 4.6°C hotter by the end of the century, with more intense and frequent heavy rainfall events, and a rise in sea levels of up to one metre.[1]

The other defining feature of this island nation is its size. Singapore is truly tiny. The entire country has a landmass of 720 square kilometres – roughly the size of New York City – with no real hinterland. Crowded into that space are seven million residents, their homes, the offices and factories they work in, and the shops and restaurants that make Singapore a culinary and retail destination.

*　*　*

Colonial Singapore had followed a well-trodden, and rather destructive, path to development. Even as far back as 1854, Wallace had grown dismayed by the deforestation in this once-luxuriant part of the world. 'Future ages will certainly look back upon us as a people so immersed in the pursuit of wealth as to be blind to higher considerations,' he wrote. 'They will charge us with having culpably allowed the destruction of some of those records of Creation which we had it in our power to preserve.' One oasis in Wallace's time might have been the Botanic Gardens, established in 1859 to promote the Victorian ideal of nature to be catalogued, observed and brought into the service of the Empire.

While the Gardens and other such colonial relics survive to this day, business logic in modern Singapore could, as in other places, have led to the paving-over of the rest of the island to house new families, provide office space for its companies and develop more of the city's famous hawker centres serving up ever more plates of fiery noodles. So it surprised me to learn that today, nearly half the island is green space – some of that managed, like parks and gardens, with the rest given over to unmanicured forests, mangroves and wetlands.[2]

Singapore can't choose to relegate nature to country clubs and national parks several hours away like other megacities do – it doesn't have the room. Instead, the 'garden city', as founding father Lee Kwan Yew dubbed it in 1967, has been forced to become a model for making space for nature when space of all sorts is at a premium.[3] The result is a landscape of walkable,

Singapore's Gardens by the Bay, one of the city's many efforts at urban greening.

tree-lined streets; parks with meandering streams and romps of otters; a national park that hosts a night safari; and forests and mangroves for hiking and kayaking. Singapore offers a vision of a supremely liveable city, protected and regulated by natural (green) as well as human (grey) infrastructure.

Few face the crippling space constraints that this tiny island nation does. If Singapore can do it, virtually every urban area should, in my mind, eventually be able to make the business case for nature within and around our cities.

Look up the term **green infrastructure** and – as we have seen before – you will find a bewildering array of definitions, many linked to water use and all rooted in the jargon of environmental policy.

'Green infrastructure uses plants, soils, landscape design, and engineered techniques to retain, absorb, and reduce polluted stormwater runoff,' the US Environmental Protection Agency says.[4] The European Environment Agency tends to see green infrastructure (GI) in broader terms. 'A wide range of environmental features that operate at different scales and form part of an interconnected ecological network [...] they must be more than simply "green spaces",' it admits, saying GI is 'designed to maintain and enhance the delivery of benefits to human society in the form of food, materials, clean water, clean air, climate regulation, flood prevention, pollination, and recreation'.[5] Persevere in the face of these buzzwords, and you will be rewarded with more terminology, including the concept of 'green–blue grids' that integrate trees and greenery with waterways and wetlands to improve the local environment and strengthen climate resilience.

All of these terms point to what is, in my mind, a simple and intuitive notion: that our conurbations can bring nature in, rather than keep it out. Doing so might take different forms – from putting green walls on buildings and trees along avenues, to restoring rivers and mangrove swamps. But at the core of this notion is an acknowledgement that many of our urban challenges, from flooding to extreme heat, stem from trying to fight nature with concrete and steel. While new technologies such as rapid-response flood defences and low-emissions air conditioners will form part of our climate adaptation toolkits, nature offers a compelling complement to these examples of human ingenuity.

Through the rest of this chapter, I'll use the term green infrastructure in the broadest possible sense: to encompass all the ways in which cities are working with, rather than against, nature. Cities across the world are beginning to reap the rewards of this approach. As we'll see, such greening doesn't just make our cities prettier and more liveable; it comes with a powerful business case that we can no longer afford to ignore.

* * *

Let's return to Singapore for a moment to take a closer look at a 150-acre oasis within its urban jungle – the Bishan-Ang Mo Kio (AMK) park.

AMK park stands on what was once a concretised river used for drainage purposes. To adapt to ever-more-intense rainfall, Singapore had a choice between upgrading the concrete canal, or stripping the concrete away and turning it back into a natural river. The city chose the latter after studying the costs and benefits of both approaches, deciding not only to provide a natural form of stormwater management, but also to transform the existing space into a recreational hub for residents and tourists.

As with everything in Singapore, work proceeded apace; the results were stunning. The re-naturalised AMK park boosted its water-carrying capacity by 40 per cent, improving flood mitigation and stormwater management, and generated a 30 per cent increase in biodiversity: sightings were recorded of many rare wildflower, bird and dragonfly species.[6] Perhaps more importantly, however, the integration of the infrastructure with the park created a vibrant, healthy green space for people to exercise, relax, socialise and connect with nature. In a neat twist, blocks from the lining of the old canal were used to build a viewing point, called Recycle Hill; climbing up the mound one hot, humid morning, I looked out onto a lush ecosystem that I could scarcely believe was in the heart of a major global city.

On the face of it, this might appear to be a case of a wealthy administration paying through the nose to beautify its environment. But it turned out that the economic case for the AMK investment was tremendously compelling, as researchers from the National University of Singapore found.

For one, the green infrastructure approach saved Singapore money. The cost of upgrading the 2.7 kilometre–long concrete canal would have been SGD$133 million, roughly USD$95 million. Re-naturalising the river and integrating it with the park cost just over half that. But the park also made Singapore more liveable – and it turns out those recreational, socio-cultural and tourism-related benefits can be quantified too. Researchers estimated that these broader economic gains added up to between USD$100–220 million annually.

Taking an even wider view, such projects, and the ecosystem services they provide to cities, can make a meaningful contribution to human welfare. In addition to attracting visitors, urban green space improves residents' mental health outcomes. Scaled up to community-level, the existence of Bishan-AMK is estimated to result in USD$59 million in annual savings on healthcare spending for Singapore's population, the figure being derived from avoided spending on mental health provision.[7]

AMK park is but one well-documented example of the many benefits that nature can offer city-dwellers; benefits that might seem diffuse at first but can add up to hundreds of millions of dollars for each project. Built infrastructure clearly has its place – Singapore might not be the business success story it is without its speedy mass transit system or those gleaming skyscrapers – but nature provides a demonstrable complement or counterbalance to grey infrastructure that can more than pay for itself over time.

Looking elsewhere in the world, I found that the shoots of urban greening were springing up everywhere and delivering a suite of benefits to residents and the urban ecology that surrounds them.

Take heat, that bane of city living that is only set to intensify with climate change. Buildings and asphalt tend to create urban heat islands that can be 1–4°C warmer on average than surrounding areas. Air conditioning only makes this problem worse, cooling the interiors of buildings but expelling heat onto the streets.

Cities across the world are finding that green roofs, green walls and trees can make a world of a difference. Toronto, for instance, has estimated that adding green cover to just 6 per cent of its roof space could lower the heat island effect by 1–2°C during summers.[8] Medellín's Green Corridors project has similarly reduced city temperatures by 2°C.[9]

As obvious as it may seem, we've seen cities across the world pave over their natural wealth; it's only when we tot up the numbers that the value of something as simple as shade becomes apparent. Sacramento County in northern California, a region that was once densely forested, now faces rising temperatures, droughts and wildfires. The urban forest that Sacramento has maintained and protected – consisting of six million trees – has been estimated to lower air conditioning use by over 10 per cent, saving residents nearly $20 million annually. Trees also absorb air pollutants, for an implied value of $28.7 million. Taken together, researchers found that each urban tree provided $90 in benefits per year – compared to the $30–35 cost of maintaining them.[10]

The improvements in air quality that urban trees bring are not to be underestimated. The Nature Conservancy, in wide-ranging, multi-country studies, found that the business case for tree planting is even stronger in developing cities haunted by the spectre of toxic air, such as Jakarta, Mexico City, Cairo and Karachi, among others. Annual investments as small as $4 per resident, over several years, could make meaningful differences and more than pay for themselves in lower healthcare costs.[11]

Above all, as in Singapore, the presence of nature simply makes cities more pleasant places to live. How do we quantify those benefits? In London, a group of organisations including the Greater London Authority and Vivid Economics, a consultancy, worked to pin down the benefits. They found that the city's green spaces helped Londoners avoid £950 million annually in healthcare costs by providing spaces to exercise. Beyond space to jog or play five-a-side football, parks naturally deliver feelings of peace and calm that busy city-dwellers often crave; the avoided costs of treating mental health challenges in London amounted to an enormous £370 million.[12]

Green infrastructure can go beyond urban centres, too: it can also replace grey infrastructure outside a city's borders that is necessary for the functioning of the urban area. The classic case of the Catskill mountains, 100 miles upstream of New York City, remains just as relevant today as it was in the 1990s. Faced with a $4–6 billion upfront bill and annual costs of $250 million to upgrade New York's water filtration system with treatment plants, the city chose instead to turn to nature. Spending less than an eighth of that figure, the city bought up and restored forested tracts of land in the Catskills, and in partnership with farmers in the area created a unique programme, Whole Farm, to reduce pollution running into the Catskills watershed. [13, 14]

Even today, the vast majority of the city's water supply remains 'unfiltered', straight from the source, kept pristine and purified along the way by natural means. The approach might not be suitable for every city, but it's clear that green infrastructure can be a sound investment, even at the vast scale of the city that never sleeps.

Perhaps the most compelling economic argument for urban nature lies in the natural ecosystems that defend cities from devastating floods and storm surges that threaten their very existence. In temperate regions, this might involve restoring floodplains and marshes. Tiny, low-lying Belgium, for instance, is restoring thousands of acres of wetlands at a cost of €600 million, with the entire project set to be complete by 2030. The alternative looks bleak: researchers found that the yearly cost of flood damage could amount to €1 billion by the end of the century in the absence of this investment in green infrastructure.[15]

In warmer climates, mangroves play a starring role in protecting coastal cities and communities. A pioneering 2020 paper in *Nature* finally put a number on the value that cities from Manila to Miami gain from mangrove-based flood protection: an astounding $65 billion.[16] Those protective attributes kicked in during particularly tough times; 90 per cent of the benefit was during tropical cyclones rather than regular rain conditions. Other estimates peg the total flood resilience benefits at as high as $80 billion globally.[17]

In a neat twist, mangroves can even help protect the built infrastructure we need for the climate transition from the ravages of a changing climate. A study by Earth Security, a consultancy, on behalf of investors in a windfarm in Pakistan found that an investment of $352,400 in mangrove regeneration would yield benefits of $7 million for the windfarm in reduced maintenance costs from flooding and generate another $7 million for local communities through project-based job creation and higher shrimp yields.[18]

The story of green infrastructure isn't just a set of successes, done and dusted, from obvious leading lights like Singapore. Rather, it's an evolving story that unfolds over decades, as cities grow and take tentative steps towards valuing urban ecology.

The fate of Mumbai, India's bustling business capital by the sea, has always been intimately tied to the tides. Early on, British colonists saw strategic advantage in its deep-water harbour, set on India's western coast and perfectly positioned for trade across the Arabian Sea. So, they took what had been a set of seven swampy islands inhabited by modest fishing communities and embarked on a vast project of dominion over nature. Starting in the late 1700s, a series of embankments were built and land was reclaimed, with – unsurprisingly for the times – little regard for the surrounding ecology. By 1838, Mumbai had become one contiguous peninsula, the foundation for a hub of commerce and industry that endures to this day. Further reclamations continued through the twentieth century, culminating with the construction of the business district of Nariman Point in the 1970s.[19]

The pressures of creeping urbanisation have hardly relented in the years since: between 1977 and 2017, Mumbai lost nearly two-thirds of its water bodies and vegetation.[20] But while natural buffers against storm surges disappeared within city limits, surrounding Mumbai there remained a vast ecosystem of mangrove swamps and wetlands that have received a degree of protection. Seen from above, Sanjay Gandhi National Park appears to embrace the city, and signs of Mumbai's wilder surroundings often make themselves known to city-dwellers. Large flocks of flamingos descend on Navi (New) Mumbai's wetlands every winter, with a record number delighting a locked-down city in the depths of the first Covid-19 wave in 2020. There is even the occasional leopard sighting in the outer suburbs, which keeps residents on their toes and reliably sends local media channels into a frenzy.

Unfortunately, these welcome glimpses of the region's biodiversity disguise an urban infrastructure that is failing its citizens. Historically high rainfall has hit the city in recent years as climate change has intensified cyclones in the Arabian Sea and shifted monsoon patterns. With urban sprawl having replaced the natural wetland and riverine sponges that once stood there, streets turn into streams and floodwaters claim lives and livelihoods with worrying intensity and frequency. It is the city's least privileged residents who bear much of the burden. The pressure looks unlikely to relent: the World Bank estimates that Mumbai will bear $6.4 billion in flood-related costs annually by 2050.[21]

Part of the answer surely lies in upgrading the city's creaking grey infrastructure. Mumbai's colonial-era stormwater

Mangrove forests in Mumbai's vicinity. © Aaran Patel, by permission.

drains are simply not fit for purpose; renewing them is a key priority. So too is the installation of walls, pumps and flood-gates to keep neighbourhoods safe. But the city's leaders and a committed group of activists, philanthropists and scientists are also looking to emulate the likes of Singapore. Bolstering the city's natural defences, rather than seeking simply to subdue nature like Mumbai's colonial masters once did, is now rightly on the agenda.

Mumbai's 2022 Climate Action Plan, a joint effort between the government, the World Resources Institute and the C40 Cities network that includes leaders like Singapore, emphasises the role of nature in addressing Mumbai's vulnerability to a changing climate. For one, the city has made urban greening and biodiversity one of six key planks of its plan, touting the benefits of greening in reducing the urban heat island effect and improving the health and wellbeing of residents. The plan also admits that the large-scale 'concretisation' of the city has exacerbated Mumbai's monsoonal woes, acknowledging that 'nature-based solutions would go a long way in reducing annual instances of waterlogging and flooding'. Looking ahead, the plan offers a detailed vulnerability analysis and a range of quantitative targets for the short and medium term.[22]

Mumbai is also banding together with other cities to bring nature back. In 2021, thirty-one cities, from Tel Aviv and Tokyo to Mumbai and Milan, signed C40's Urban Nature Declaration. In it, they each committed to using their city budgets and policy tools to achieve 30–40 per cent green cover by 2030, and to ensuring that 70 per cent of residents were no more than a fifteen-minute walk or bike ride from green or blue spaces.

Aaditya Thackeray, the then–Minister for Environment & Climate Change for the state, described Mumbai's C40 commitment as core to the city's climate action plan. 'Climate change is the greatest inequity – the ones least responsible are most affected,' he said at the launch, hoping that Mumbai could be 'a shining example of how diverse ecosystems can thrive in urban environments to achieve inclusive climate resilience for all.'[23]

Freetown, the capital of Sierra Leone, had flood resilience in mind too when it signed the declaration, seeking to reverse the deforestation that had caused devastating mudslides in recent years. '"Freetown the Treetown" is our city's ambitious plan to plant and grow one million trees over two rainy seasons,' Mayor Yvonne Aki-Sawyerr said. 'But we're not only planting them, we're growing them – which means we're monitoring their growth, and bringing new life to our hillsides and mangrove-forested areas.'[24]

Lubaina Rangwala of the World Resources Institute, one of the authors of Mumbai's climate action plan, told me that the emphasis on restoring nature to Mumbai reflected a far broader shift in thinking across different stakeholder groups in the city. 'There's a completely different conversation that is now active in the city. And it's not only the leaders that are leading it – it's the citizenry too, demanding changes to our post-independence love of concrete and steel. The business case for nature's impact on health and infrastructure was becoming clearer by the day.'

She told me that the updated thinking also reflected an acknowledgement of the city's past. 'The entire city has been built over a delta [...] over mudflats and wetlands. What does it mean to be able to return some of these to their original state, and to bring back the natural flood resilience that the city used to have at one point? It means rethinking what the aesthetic of modern development looks like.'

In *Bombay Imagined*, a meticulously researched compendium of the unbuilt projects that litter Mumbai's urban planning history, Robert Stephens highlights several earlier efforts to rethink the urban fabric of the city, from a proposal to create a Central Park-style green space in the place of a colonial-era racecourse in the heart of the city (an initiative that, one government advisor suggested to me, might yet see the light of day) to an aviary to bring vultures back to the Zoroastrian Towers of Silence.

But Stephens' book begins at the very beginning, in 1670, when Governor Gerald Aungier weighed the construction of a city on the Isle of Bombay. 'It is a matter of great importance and will certainly raise discontent in the inhabitants when their trees shall be cut down and destroyed,' Aungier wrote, reflecting the reticence of the nature-dependent local populace at the time. Mumbaikars are no less dependent on nature than they were all those years ago; the city's future will depend, in part, on the extent to which they can fashion a new nature-centric urbanism in the years to come.

As with every case for nature that, on examination, appears to be blindingly self-evident, a familiar question springs to mind. Why is green infrastructure, broadly defined, still the exception in our cities?

For one, cities rarely undergo carefully planned, forward-looking development of the sort that Singapore was lucky to have.[25] Part of what makes our urban agglomerations so dynamic is the entrepreneurial energy and grit of new migrants. But many cities have had decades or centuries of haphazard expansion. At each stage, it might have been more profitable to drain a wetland or raze a forest to make way for such growth; green roofs might understandably have been a lower priority than roofs in the first place. But it's never too late to bring nature back in, even if it's been banished from the city limits for generations. This is just as true in the developing world, in places like Mumbai and Medellín, as it is in 2,000-year-old London.

A very real challenge is the urban planning orthodoxy that prizes large, grey projects that can generate headlines (and in some cases, kickbacks for officials) over simpler green approaches. This feeds through to financing. To be fair, green infrastructure isn't widely understood, and it can be tricky to measure and predict the effectiveness of such projects. Local decision-makers often lack quantifiable data that is relevant for urban planning in their region. For all the success stories, these approaches remain the exception, and a lack of trust and familiarity in addition to uncertainty over cost-effectiveness can cause planners (and the army of consultants that advises them) to gravitate towards the default option.[26]

A related challenge is the short-term nature of public and private decision-making in cities. Green infrastructure projects often require multi-decade planning and maintenance for their benefits to be fully realised. Such delayed gratification can sit uneasily with the appraisal cycles of officials or business leaders, optimising as they do for re-election or annual reporting.[27]

Then there is the question of how to pay for green infrastructure investments, and who captures the benefits that accrue. With grey infrastructure, developers are able to fund construction with a suite of financial tools: roads can be paid for with tolls or local taxes, and water treatment plants with user charges. Cities find it straightforward to borrow money or raise project funding against these future cash flows, readily financed by traditional infrastructure investors and banks.

But the public goods of nature are often inherently public, and the benefits cannot be monetised by any one party. No wonder that there aren't major green infrastructure developers, ready to bid on tenders for mangrove restoration or public park construction and then execute and maintain these projects for decades. Governments come closest to being able to capture benefits like lower healthcare costs and disaster relief spending, which we now know to be substantial. So, unlike other business cases, this one might be most relevant to the public sector, even if there is room to innovate with private sources of funding.[28]

But even forward-looking city governments face many barriers. A detailed 2020 study by the European Commission found that cities such as Glasgow, Turin and Eindhoven had struggled on a number of fronts, despite policymakers having taken initial decisions to invest in green infrastructure. Beyond a lack of qualified suppliers and in-house skills and expertise within the private sector, the report's authors also highlighted many institutional and legal barriers, rooted in traditional paradigms of grey infrastructure.[29]

Encouragingly, there are efforts afoot to help policymakers structure urban investments into nature, much as an army of consultants and financiers readily do for grey infrastructure. In 2022, the Nature Conservancy and Pegasys, a consultancy, launched the Nature4Water facility, which has been 'purpose-built to provide the gold standard in technical assistance to help local champions build out watershed investment programs'.[30]

Oliver Karius, CEO of LGT Venture Philanthropy and one of the supporters of Nature4Water, described why this was an attractive proposition to city administrators. 'I come from South Africa, and we have Day Zero in Cape Town when the city runs out of water. [Rather than invest in] reverse osmosis with diesel generators or whatever to provide water, the science for investing in nature has been there for a long time in Cape Town, but they had not built the business case for it. The Nature Conservancy helped to actually develop the business case that the removal of invasive species in the catchment areas around Cape Town would free up two months of fresh water for Cape Town at a tenth of the cost.' It is interventions like these that the Nature4Water team is looking to accelerate. 'Once you make the case, with evidence, then people say, "Hang on, let's look into this – it makes economic sense!"'

But it's worth considering whether green infrastructure *is* in fact widespread but merely unacknowledged. The cases highlighted in this chapter involved cities taking proactive steps to bring nature into the urban fold. But even in those that don't, nature, whether incidental or vestigial, continues quietly to serve residents. Those cooling, purifying, flood-defending benefits just aren't part of the calculus that public and private entities use to value the spaces they govern and inhabit. In the next chapter, we'll see how the overarching framework of natural capital might allow us to take stock of such benefits, and finally bring them into the narrow economic thinking that continues to dominate. For now, pausing to acknowledge these diffuse natural benefits that make cities liveable is a start.

To my mind, the next decade holds tremendous promise for the re-greening of the world's cities as more places tot up the costs and benefits, and partners in the private and non-profit sectors develop the expertise to support cities.

The first, and most obvious step, is for cities to protect what they already have in and around their borders. Quantifying the benefits of standing wetlands, mangroves and forests is already underway. That alone should provide a powerful business case for protection, starting today, even if it means turning down short-term profit and building denser, greener urban cores rather than resigning ourselves to endless suburban sprawl. Singapore's case remains instructive here: without the option of sprawling into the countryside, the city has turned itself into a model of restraint and clever densification even as it sets aside a large chunk of surrounding land for conservation.

But as they look to build the urban infrastructure of the future, city leaders and their residents need to consider grey and green options as genuine equals. This should begin with the demands that we citizens make of local officials after every flood or heatwave. Rather than reflexively asking for upgrades to canals or seawalls, why not demand our leaders to consider green alternatives? The inverse of that should be reflected in the procurement processes that cities use so they encourage green alternatives to be pitched for every traditional project they consider. According to the European Commission this challenge-based procurement could involve 'specifying only desired outcomes in the call for tenders and asking suppliers to come up with their ideas on how to address those'.[31]

A dash of creativity can also help when it comes to the ghosts of grey infrastructure past. New York's High Line, a stunning elevated park and walking path, was built in 2009 on a disused train line. Encouragingly, the project came about through a grassroots movement, coordinated by non-profit group Friends of the High Line that continues to maintain the park in partnership with the city. Other cities have employed similar thinking to revitalise old, hulking concrete structures, perhaps none more audaciously than Madrid. Where a highway once cut through the heart of the city there now stands a beautiful green space, Madrid Rio, that provides new lungs to this ancient city.

The fact that some greening initiatives can begin hyper-locally, at the level of the neighbourhood rather than at City Hall, should give us hope; over time, inspiration might even be found in these pockets within cities rather than halfway across the world. As such, inviting communities into green infrastructure planning is another no-brainer – something that should be at the heart of all urban planning going forward. At their best, green spaces bring neighbourhoods and communities together, creating well-paid jobs both in embedding green infrastructure and maintaining it over the long term. To that end, consultation at every stage of the process can help create the buy-in and public access communities need to make the most of these initiatives. Just like grey infrastructure, the green sort can lie underutilised too; it would be a shame to replace one sort of white elephant project with another.

We must do a better job of sharing the benefits of urban greening. Like most other types of urban infrastructure, access to green infrastructure is steeped in inequality. One study by American Forests, a non-profit, showed that predominantly minority neighbourhoods have on average 33 per cent less tree cover than majority-white ones, while the poorest have 41 per cent less canopy than the wealthiest; another by Friends of the Earth in the UK found a strong correlation between green space deprivation, and both ethnicity and income.[32,33]

This unedifying pattern plays out in cities across the world; we need to design future urban greening initiatives with equity in mind.

Finally, it's important to be clear on the capacity of green infrastructure in the context of a changing climate. Green infrastructure can be an effective buffer against rising temperatures and sea levels, but even natural defences have their limits and will sometimes break. Planning ahead is sensible, but cities will need to accept these limitations and continue to invest in thoroughly decarbonising their buildings, energy and transportation systems.

If a city-state as small as Singapore can bring back some of the wild side that Wallace once experienced, then other urban areas can surely follow its lead, and build greener, healthier, and more resilient futures for their residents in the process. Nature belongs in our cities just as much as it does in our forests and seas.

Natural Capital: A Framework

We've examined several cases for nature up close and seen how they can matter for us and our planet; now let's turn our attention to natural capital, the framework that underpins them. We're all familiar with the idea of economic capital, even if we don't always call it that. Capital comes in many shapes and sizes, and it includes the cash in our wallets, the value of our homes, factories and cars, the balance sheets of businesses and the budgets of governments. Money makes the world go round, and we've used it to create an entire economic system – more akin to an unacknowledged ideology than a simple framework – that we now call capitalism.

Plenty has been written about the history of modern capitalism since its emergence in the early nineteenth century in Western Europe: from its precedents in mercantilism in the seventeenth and eighteenth centuries, to post-war tussles with communism, to the resurgence of free-market thinking in the form of neoliberalism in the 1980s and a more recent push to temper capitalism's worst impacts on people and the planet. You may already have your own views on the merits and demerits of capitalism. My own view is that financial capitalism has done a commendable job with the creation of wealth and an appalling one with its distribution, but there are many excellent works of scholarship from writers far more qualified than I am to comment on the matter.

The framework that financial capitalism provides has historically been a tremendously useful tool for individuals, businesses and governments to manage their resources and balance the books. Two concepts lie at the core of this usefulness – stocks and flows.

Measuring our capital *stocks* allows us to figure out how much our assets are worth in economic terms at some point in time. If you're lucky enough to own a house, you'll have some sense of what the market will pay for it now, and how the value of that stock of capital has changed or will change over time. For a business, capital stocks might include the value of its factories and the goods it produces and stores in inventory. Knowing what these are worth is essential to understanding underlying financial health.

Then there are flows of capital that make up what statisticians call 'economic activity'. For a house, the flow of capital might include the rent you get from letting it out and the payments you make to a mortgage provider. For a business, flows can come from the cash they earn when they sell their goods, and the cash they pay out to the workers who make them. Together, stocks and flows of economic capital paint a picture of what's going on in the modern market economy – whether we're getting richer or poorer in the stocks we hold, and whether the flows are at appropriate levels relative to those stocks.

The same stocks-and-flows thinking applies to natural capital. Take a population of trees in a rainforest in Borneo, for example. These trees would be considered a natural capital asset, or stock, while the timber that can be harvested from them would be a provisioning service, or flow. Alternatively, consider a fishery in the North Atlantic: those schools of haddock, cod and mackerel represent a stock, and provide a flow in the form of the fishing industry's catch every year.[1]

Natural capital is simply the framework that brings these stocks and flows together. The Natural Capital Forum calls it 'the world's stocks of natural assets which include geology, soil, air, water and all living things'.[2] Nature capital assets, like forests or oceans, in turn provide flows, or **ecosystem services**, which generate societal benefits and contribute to human health and wellbeing.

Flows of ecosystem services can be converted to financial capital. To date, we've largely valued and monetised the flows of physical natural commodities, like timber or fish; an excessive focus on just these ecosystem services has been at the root of unchecked destruction. This book, and natural capital economics as a whole, is about valuing a wider swathe of services – from climate stabilisation to pollination – and turning the protection and restoration of both these flows and their underlying stocks into economic benefits for communities.

The UK government's Natural Capital Committee also emphasises the usefulness of these flows to human society. It writes that 'natural capital [is] that part of nature which directly or indirectly underpins value to people, including ecosystems, species, freshwater, soils, minerals, the air and oceans, as well as natural processes and functions'.[3]

The Intergovernmental Science-Policy Platform on Biodiversity and Ecosystem Services (IPBES) uses the refreshingly direct acronym NCP (nature's contribution to people) to build on ecosystem services, emphasising 'the central role that culture plays in defining NCP [...] especially the complementarity between scientific, indigenous, and local knowledge'.[4]

Later we will explore indigenous and local knowledge and how these forms of knowledge interact with natural capital thinking but, for now, you may be wondering: why is this framework, which might seem like the preserve of green entrepreneurs and policy wonks, relevant to the rest of us? Because it finally gives us the language to describe and value what might be clear to you by now: the many seen and often-unseen benefits we enjoy from nature.

Gretchen Daily is the Director of the Stanford Natural Capital Project (NatCap) and perhaps one of the world's foremost scientists engaged in the work of valuing nature. When I joined her for lunch in her pretty Palo Alto garden, we sat surrounded by native plants and grasses and buzzing bees; a gnarled persimmon tree was heavy with bounty; the family dog pawed the grass beneath. The crisp February air felt like a freely given privilege after some of the worst California wildfire seasons on record.

We were there to talk about the unifying framework – natural capital – that she and her team have been instrumental in developing. 'One way to think about it is to think of all these billionaires blasting off into space – what would they need to live on Mars?' Gretchen told me. 'When I try and make natural capital tangible, I think of all that humanity would need to take to build a thriving ecosystem on another planet.'

Gretchen's pioneering work, some of it conducted in partnership with legendary ecologist Paul Ehlrich, focused on describing and delineating these ecosystem services that we now classify into four types: provisioning, regulating, supporting and cultural services.

Provisioning services are the most obvious ones – like that timber from Borneo or those fish from Iceland. Humans have always kept themselves fed, clothed and sheltered with nature's bounty. Nor are these services limited to domesticated species; IPBES found that humans rely on as many as 50,000 wild species, with one in five people directly dependent on wild plants, animals and fungi for their food and income.[5] Nature also provides us with other, less obvious provisions, like medicinal plants. The US Forest Service estimates that 40 per cent of the drugs you'd find in a pharmacy are derived from plants – many based on knowledge that indigenous cultures have relied on for millennia.[6]

Provisioning services are the ones most likely to be priced and traded on the open market, and have consumptive, direct use values. Overall, that value is likely woefully incomplete: who knows how many other medicinal plants are out there waiting to be discovered by modern medicine? But the other three classes of ecosystem services are even further from being valued, and the vast majority of their benefits remain invisible to decision-makers. Despite nature offering us clear benefits beyond consumptive services, they are rarely valued in monetary terms and their value is only truly appreciated once they are lost.

Take **regulating services** – the many things nature does to make our planet liveable. Nature draws down carbon, as we saw in Colombia; it filters the air and water, as we saw in Singapore and New York; it holds back storm surges, as we saw in Mumbai. Elsewhere, pollinators work tirelessly to ensure the circle of life continues, with important financial implications for our food system: studies have found that a single bee colony can sustain yearly agricultural production worth up to $1,050, a service that in the US alone was worth $34 billion in 2012, or roughly $44 billion in 2022 dollars.[7, 8]

Third come the **cultural services** that make our living planet worth living for. Think of the central role that nature plays in religions and spiritual traditions the world over, the joy it provides the hiker or diver, the peace it gives a stressed-out office worker strolling through a city park. Some of these values can be inferred in the form of real estate price premiums, lower mental health spending and a willingness to pay for ecotourism. The majority of cultural services may not fit narrow economic thinking; as we'll see in the chapter on the indigenous case for nature, we should never lose sight of a more profound intrinsic case for nature. But even the narrow sliver that can be valued makes for a hugely compelling economic story.

Finally, there are the **supporting services** – the basic building blocks of biology, physics and chemistry – that make life on earth possible. From photosynthesis to nutrient cycling, these lay the foundation for all the other services that we've come to rely on.

To be clear, not all of nature's impacts are benign with respect to us. There are indeed ecosystem disservices, from weeds on farms, to plagues of locusts and forest fires that choke the air with smoke. But it's important to recognise that for much of human history, nature essentially regulated itself. The trouble came when growing numbers of us began demanding ever more of these services of nature – and in doing so, threw the balance of the planet's ecosystems totally out of whack. Picture a trust-fund family attempting to live off the interest from the account while simultaneously drawing down the principal, even as more spendthrift children join the fray. Many of the disservices we see today are really a reflection of our similarly shameful record in managing stocks and flows of natural capital: an endowment that was given to us by the planet, which we have squandered.

Natural capital thinking of this sort allows us to examine questions of sustainability. Can we afford to keep going down this path, razing forests and emptying the seas at a wildly unsustainable rate? Clearly not. But how much is too much? Taking a look at the *stocks* can show us the way; Palau's fisheries, for example, have rebounded precisely because the proportion of the flow (the catch) captured by humans has returned to sustainable levels relative to the underlying fish population.

How does natural capital relate to markets? The Taskforce on Nature Markets, established in 2022, defines a nature market as one where 'the transacted good or service specifically reflects a stock of ecosystem assets or a flow of ecosystem services from terrestrial or aquatic ecosystems'.[9]

I like to think of natural capital as the thread that links the many business cases for nature, some of which we have examined in this book. Carbon markets? They're finally valuing the regulating climate service that nature provides. Ecotourism?

It simply provides a way for communities to earn a living from the cultural services of the ecosystems that they inhabit. Nature-positive agriculture? It replenishes the stock of natural capital in our soils, so they can help regulate our environment and give us more sustainable flows of food over time.

In laying out the state of nature markets, the Taskforce point out that the largest ones, centred around food and commodities, are also the oldest, even as new ones around cultural or carbon value emerge. They also highlight what we know to be true: that these markets are subject to malign forces much like any other markets, estimating that nature crimes including illegal mining, poaching and deforestation account for $280 billion a year.[10] We cannot wish away the existence of such forces; governance, as with any other market, will be vitally important to promote good behaviour and punish malfeasance.

The cases and markets we've covered are by no means comprehensive. Others will surely be discovered and expanded upon over time as we wake up to the true value of nature. But failing to account for the full value of ecosystems has resulted in the vast underappreciation of the benefits we glean from our natural world. By illuminating the economic value that we currently ignore, the natural capital framework can be a powerful corrective.

To Ricardo Bayon, a pioneer of environmental markets, our system of financial capitalism was necessary but no longer sufficient. 'The financial system we've created is an incredibly powerful tool. Probably one of the most powerful tools that humans have ever created. But the problem was that it was created in a very different time, a very different world. One where natural resources were plentiful and capital and labour were scarce. I think that's flipping. So, scarcity drives value. Natural resources are becoming scarcer and therefore more valuable!'

'If we can't make the economic case for nature... then we are all on a suicidal course,' Gretchen Daily said. 'And we're going to stay on that course until we make that case as widely as possible.'

Beyond valuing individual ecosystem services, some have attempted to estimate the value of all of the planet's natural capital. As far back as 1997, Robert Constanza, Rudolf de Groot and others pegged the value of global ecosystem services at $16–54 trillion in 1994 US dollars, the equivalent of between $32-109tn in 2022 dollars. A more recent effort by the same duo put the figure at $130tn in 2010 dollars; $178tn in today's money.[11]

Remember that these estimates relate to flows, not stocks. To provide a point of comparison, the IMF estimated that global dollar GDP, our preferred, if deeply flawed, measure of global economic flows, was $94 trillion in 2021.[12] If the figures seem enormous, they also seem broadly consistent with the indisputable fact that human life on earth could not exist without nature.

Shouldn't they be even bigger, or perhaps even infinite, considering the existential nature of clean air or water to human society? Perhaps, but such valuation methods can only ever capture a fraction of the total value – some of it beyond the realm of economics – that our ecosystems provide. Using a consistent method can at least show the direction in which natural capital stocks and flows are trending, a useful lens to apply if we're mostly concerned with managing them for sustainability over the long term.

It can be easier to digest these colossal figures if we take them down a level to individual countries. And few countries have done more to take stock of their natural capital than the UK, with teams from the Office of National Statistics (ONS) undertaking an exercise of rare sophistication to make sense of the value of the UK's urban green spaces, farmland, forests and coasts.

The ONS found, with characteristic linguistic precision, that in 2019 'the stock of the aspects of UK natural capital we can currently value was estimated to be worth £1.2 trillion'. Interestingly, over half that stock value came from cultural services, the vast majority in the form of tourism and recreation. Regulating services, including carbon storage, air pollutant removal and urban cooling amounted to about £175 billion, while £357 billion came from the provisioning of water, fuel, food and the like.[13]

In 2021, the UK Treasury released a complementary piece of work, the Dasgupta Review on the Economics of

Biodiversity, that set out a new framework for how governments could think about the economics of nature. The review was led by Professor Sir Partha Dasgupta, a Cambridge economist who now rejects his discipline's narrow-minded focus on produced capital. Running to over 600 pages, it is by far the most comprehensive effort to date to examine the relationship between biodiversity and economics.[14]

'Our notion of nature is often one of amenity [...] A lovely walk, a mountain climb and so on. But our economic relationship with nature [...] is full of missing markets and moral hazard,' Sir Partha told me when we met in his wood-panelled study, expressing the hope that the review would give businesses and policymakers the language they need to rethink that relationship. He had found a willing audience for his ideas within the British political establishment and had spent the last several months disseminating his findings at hundreds of events, lectures and hearings. 'What was interesting to me was how informed the parliamentarians were in the UK. They were very, very informed, and they had very intelligent questions to ask!'

The Biden administration has begun similar efforts to measure the United States' natural capital, releasing a draft national strategy in late 2022 to 'reflect natural assets on America's balance sheet'. The strategy recommended that the government 'produce a new, ongoing set of statistics to take stock of our wealth of natural assets, how those assets are being enhanced or depleted, and the impact that has on our economic strength'.[15]

Halfway across the world, China – a huge carbon emitter and to date a climate laggard – is finally showing a degree of leadership on the natural capital front. In a quest to transform its industrial society into an 'ecological civilization', it is identifying crucial areas for securing nature and its vital benefits to people, with 50 per cent of the country now zoned to limit human activity. Some Chinese provinces have taken the lead on piloting a new metric pioneered by Gretchen Daily and her team, Gross Environmental Product, as an alternative to Gross Domestic Product, which is the standard *flow* measure of economic activity over a given time period. Relying solely on GDP for national accounts is clearly incomplete; GEP helps correct that myopia by measuring the total value of ecosystem goods and services supplied to human wellbeing in a region annually. Despite these high-profile examples, governments are yet to truly integrate natural capital into their economic planning, and GEP is nowhere close to replacing GDP measurements. Leading economists acknowledge that GDP is flawed but policymakers can't agree on what to replace it with.

If governments are being slow to find consensus and take action, perhaps businesses could lead the way – particularly in places that face greater constraints on policy-making than China? It can indeed be useful to assess natural capital in the context of a business and its supply chain. Puma, the sportswear manufacturer, published an environmental profit and loss account in 2011, while Unilever took steps to integrate natural capital into its supply chain in 2014. But progress on this front has been markedly slower than on carbon accounting. A McKinsey report in 2022 found that 83 per cent of Fortune Global 500 companies had set a specific climate target, compared to just 5 per cent for biodiversity loss.[16] Few high-profile cases exist on comprehensive natural capital reporting, even as hundreds of companies, for instance, make vague pledges to be nature-positive or end deforestation in their supply chains.

A lack of investor and public pressure for progress on nature might be one culprit for the plodding pace. Another might be a simple lack of expertise. 'One of the things I've been trying to push to CEOs whom I've been talking to over the last year is that they should hire ecologists,' Sir Partha said. 'We [economists] are the ones who have infiltrated everything, you know. But how can companies ever know about the state of ecosystems from which they're importing raw materials without people who understand those systems?'

There is also a problem of standardisation. 'Climate change has the benefit of being reduced to a single parameter: carbon emissions,' Sir Partha said. 'From carbon emissions comes [atmospheric] concentration… temperature rise… and the effects on people. But I'm old enough to remember that getting [to that understanding] took many, many years.'

Putting a value on nature, of course, requires us to track a vast variety of ecosystem services that are far from interchangeable. Carbon emissions offer a single point of focus for sustainability-minded investors and voters. But holding decision-makers' feet to the fire on creating a genuinely nature-positive economy or supply chain means tracking dozens of important metrics, from forest cover and reef health to ecosystem services in farms and urban areas.

The lack of standardisation also makes itself felt in the hazy state of current nature-related accounting rules, but there are plans afoot to surmount this challenge. The global Taskforce on Nature-Related Financial Disclosures (TNFD) is one such effort, modelled along the lines of a similar body set up to promote consistency in climate reporting. Established in 2021, the group of up to thirty-five taskforce members representing entities with a footprint in over 180 countries aims to create a framework for 'worldwide consistency for nature-related reporting' for financial institutions and companies. Public consultations on promising beta versions of its framework are being carried out; the hope is ultimately that the TNFD will set a transparent, widely accepted standard for how businesses can quantify the risks associated with biodiversity loss, and the negative impacts associated with their activities and operations.[17]

If this all sounds terribly staid, it's also tremendously important. Fixing the hidden plumbing of the financial system with better accounting and disclosure standards was a vital part of making the market economy work following the Great Depression. Shining a light on the hidden impacts that nature has on businesses, and that businesses have on nature, could drive a long overdue shift in global financial flows towards nature-positive outcomes.

Natural capital is certainly overlooked, but it is important to see it as part of a broader reimagination of the notion of capital. Some, including the Capitals Coalition, argue that we should consider four different kinds of capital: natural, social, human and produced. Others say there are five, splitting produced capital into financial forms (such as money) and manufactured forms (machinery, for example). Such exercises in broadening our definition of capital – in essence, expanding our collective view of what is important in the economy – are intended to 'address the three interconnected global crises of climate change, nature loss, and rising inequality', according to the Coalition.[18]

The Coalition gives an example of a manufacturer providing training to encourage food waste reduction: this practice invests people with new skills (boosting human capital), reduces costs of waste treatment (boosting produced capital), creates a sense of shared value among workers (social capital) and reduces the harmful impact of waste (natural capital). Stylised examples can only go so far, but the core idea is a sound one. The crises our societies face can't be solved in isolation; we won't get progress on nature if we don't take care of people along the way.

In addition to government and industry efforts to integrate natural capital into mainstream economic thinking, development finance institutions are stepping into the fray to support policymakers, companies and private investors. The Inter-American Development Bank, for instance, has set up a Natural Capital Lab to innovate on natural capital financing, attempting to bridge the gap between business and government action, and provide some measure of financial innovation, which we will come back to in detail in a later chapter.

But governments, businesses and international organisations have all preached the language of sustainable development for decades, even as the world burned. Is this time really any different?

'These development-oriented institutions have in the past actually been the ones at the forefront of destroying nature, often with the view that, okay, we'll transform this natural asset into something productive and help a country develop [in economic terms],' Gretchen Daily admitted. 'But now they really are shifting their view, after some devastating decades, to one that recognises the irreplaceable and absolutely critical value nature holds. We need them to deliver near-term home runs that inspire others to try the same and build confidence in the [natural capital] approach.'

* * *

For all the obvious value of natural capital, it's undeniable that this value can be fuzzy and somewhat hard to quantify. But what if we had markets for other ecosystem services beyond carbon? What if biocredits, building on the frameworks laid down for carbon credits, could value individual units of natural capital and create a market that can fund their protection?

It turns out that nature-based credits, of a kind, have been around for decades. In the early 1980s, a wetland mitigation banking system emerged in the US following the passage of the Clean Water Act.[19] By the turn of the millennium, hundreds of mitigation banks were operating across the country. These conservation banks were rooted in the creation or restoration of wetland habitats in one area to offset the loss of wetlands elsewhere, in effect forcing real estate developers or mining companies to make up for the damage they caused to a specific sort of natural capital.

In the late 1990s, complementary 'conservation banking' markets took shape, centred around (re)creating habitats for specific endangered species. In the UK, analogous efforts have focused on threatened species such as the Great Crested Newt; property developers, for instance, now routinely pay to create new ponds or shelters for the little salamanders when construction endangers existing habitats. Today, the UK is adopting a 'biodiversity net gain' framework, going beyond compensation to ask companies that damage a habitat to show that their mitigation efforts have a positive, rather than neutral, impact on the species they threaten.[20]

The Paulson Institute estimates that these biodiversity offset markets are worth $6–9 billion globally: not small change by any means.[21] But these legacy markets, rooted as they are in a *legal* framework that compensates for harm by specific project developers, and limited to damage done within the borders of a small number of advanced economies with long-denuded biodiversity, are of limited value in protecting and restoring natural capital at large. Crucially, they are process-based, largely involving the (re)creation of habitats, rather than outcome-based for species diversity and ecosystem functioning.

Some contend that a new, international, voluntary biocredit market, modelled on the rapidly growing carbon market but learning from its shortcomings, might be one way to drive more funding for conservation.

Ricardo Bayon, who co-wrote an authoritative 2007 book on conservation banking and was involved in setting up a number of biodiversity offset markets, opined on the challenges of standardising biodiversity units.

'Commoditisation is not something you have with biodiversity markets […] a snow leopard is not the same as an eagle. They're vastly different things. So it's not a [single] natural commodity,' Bayon said, echoing Sir Partha Dasgupta's reflections on the benefits of being able to reduce climate change to a single parameter. Legacy mitigation banks got around this challenge thanks to their focus on recreating the same habitats in roughly the same region, but this approach is no longer workable when looking to create international biodiversity markets that will require some common unit of measurement.

Bayon pointed out that not all markets need to follow the lead of oil or wheat, setting benchmark prices for traded commodities that are essentially identical in their characteristics. The real estate market, for instance, functions without such standardisation. It uses a common metric – square feet – but allows a square foot of property in Hong Kong to trade at a vastly higher price than the same square footage in Athens. These new biocredit schemes could do the same, with a fully restored forest in Costa Rica naturally worth more in 'biodiversity gain' terms than degraded grassland in the Brazilian *cerrado*.

One way to get around the challenge of standardisation would be to accept the diversity of nature and therefore abandon the concept of equivalence. Legacy conservation banking and carbon offset schemes are typically based on equating pollution or damage in one place with the balancing effect of positive action elsewhere. But a new paradigm is possible. The United Nations and the International Institute for Environment and Development have recommended setting up 'biocredit' schemes that do not function like offsets, and instead represent 'an entirely positive contribution to biodiversity'.[22]

They cite the work of biodiversity and climate research association Operation Wallacea, where researchers such as it's founder, Tim Coles, have suggested that baskets of biodiversity metrics – akin to the notional baskets of goods used to calculate fluctuation in the retail price index – might help quantify biodiversity gains. By tracking changes in a few locally relevant metrics – say, in the case of a recovering reef, coral cover, microorganism diversity from eDNA sampling, and fish diversity from video analysis – we might then be able to construct and trade biocredits on the basis of improvements in the index. In Operation Wallacea's methodology, a biocredit equates to a 1 per cent uplift or avoided loss in the average value of the chosen basket of metrics on a per-hectare basis. Pilot projects are already underway in the UK, Mexico, Honduras and elsewhere.[23]

These new methods will rely on our ability to understand and track the incredible complexity of ecological systems. In the following chapter, we will explore in detail how improved and emerging technologies can support such tracking in ways that would have been unimaginable to the ecologists of previous generations.

To my mind, the real value of this wave of interest in biodiversity-related credit mechanisms is the emphasis on rigorously verified outcomes. Too many of the stories that corporations tell us about nature-positive business models feel good but lack substance. If they can fund nature restoration without the pretence of equivalence, instead quantifying the 'uplift' in biodiversity outcomes in both regulated and voluntary markets, we could create a new pathway to supporting the recovery of natural capital in ecosystems of all sorts while avoiding the poor monitoring and inflated claims that eroded trust in the early days of the voluntary carbon markets.

Over time, such a system might allow the transparent stacking of various ecosystem services – say, water filtration on top of carbon value. Stacking would allow us to value each ecosystem service separately and then add them all up, rather than treating ecosystem value as a co-benefit whose effect on the credit prices is unclear. While we're not quite there yet, on either the construction or trading of biocredits, for those who care about biodiversity – and hopefully that's all of us – this is a field worth following closely in the months and years to come.

While these efforts to develop and refine the instruments of natural capital are underway, among ecology thinkers and activists there is a swathe of opinion that questions the very notion. The broad critique is that natural capital thinking is at odds with nature's intrinsic value. George Monbiot, a writer who clearly cares deeply for the natural world, remarks: 'Deluded is the expectation that we can defend the living world through the mindset that's destroying it. The notions that nature exists to serve us; that its value consists of the instrumental benefits we can extract; that this value can be measured in cash terms; and that what can't be measured does not matter, have proved lethal to the rest of life on Earth.'[24, 25]

Bram Büscher, another critic, has argued that extrinsic motivations might obscure the moral and spiritual reasons we might have to preserve nature.[26]

Later, I look closely at indigenous notions of and interactions with nature, and I share the deep conviction that nature is ultimately priceless. But, to me, natural capital thinking is an obvious complement to, not a contradiction of, that conviction. Gretchen Daily, too, had been thinking about the interplay between the natural capital approach and these nobler instincts.

'First off, I'm personally very moved by the intrinsic value sort of case [...] and I hope that we can cultivate much more awareness and understanding of the many cultures that existed until this pretty recent period of commercialising and financialising everything in life. But we've made almost no perceptible headway in averting ecosystem collapse. I feel we're doomed if we restrict ourselves to the more spiritual and intrinsic value arguments. I've seen in my own life, now that I am in my fifties, plenty of trying, by many dear friends, to rely solely on that intrinsic case. I now feel that the traction we need is more likely to come from making everybody aware of their own short-term stake in nature for their own wellbeing.'

I agree. My own view, contrary to that of its critics, is that natural capital thinking in no way implies that what can't be measured doesn't matter. It simply sets a floor price, of sorts, on nature's full economic value. And it's important to remember that nature markets already exist; it's just that they have, as currently constructed, enabled centuries of destruction by valuing nature incorrectly.

Part of the objection of environmental thinkers like Monbiot to natural capital stems from its translation of nature's value to a financial price, and a perceived implication that it can therefore be substituted by other forms of capital. 'In pricing a river, a landscape or an ecosystem, either you are lining it up for sale, in which case the exercise is sinister, or you are not, in which case it is meaningless,' Monbiot writes.

Daily pointed out that the dollar value we assign is in some ways beside the point. 'What it comes down to is just comparing options in some consistent way, and using a monetary metric is one way of making it consistent. The usefulness of such comparisons is essentially as old as human civilisation; indeed, the earliest form of writing, cuneiform, evolved in Mesopotamia as a dead simple way to account for the grain that the earliest agrarian societies were beginning to produce and trade.' Then, as now, accounting, whether in dollars or bushels of wheat, remains an essential way to create common language around what we value.

'You can absolutely take a more sophisticated approach with multiple values at play, and compare scenarios,' Daily added, keenly aware of the tricky trade-offs when dealing with natural capital, rather than entirely fungible financial capital. 'Often there will be some disagreement and some winners and losers, but often it's possible through these engagements to find a path that satisfies a broader range of stakeholders than the status quo.'

Beyond this pragmatic attitude espoused by Daily, I take issue with the assertion that such exercises are either sinister or meaningless. No natural capital accountant carries out these assessments with destruction in mind – they are virtually always an attempt to put previously hidden value on the books and make a case for protection. In any case, bad actors have never needed natural capital assessments to justify destruction: the conceptual door to the sinister exploitation of nature has long been open, with or without natural capital thinking.

Nor is natural capital valuation meaningless if there is no immediate threat to a natural ecosystem. Making a business case can help pay for both continued protection and gradual regeneration: both worthy causes in a world where economic self-interest from businesses, governments and individuals can align with what's right for nature far more often than we tend to believe.

A related criticism is that natural capital thinking could be used to privatise nature and turn what should be managed for the common good into private profit. One response is that many natural capital assessments take place at the country level; it's often the state that is best placed to capture the public-goods-style benefits of diffuse ecosystem services in the form of lower disaster relief or health spending. Natural capital accounts can enable them to take a long, hard look at the condition of their ecosystems and identify areas where protection and regeneration make economic as well as moral sense. Another is that it's already possible to privatise nature: private farmers, ranchers and forest owners are mostly free to do what they want on immense swathes of the planet. The trouble is that the current paradigm pushes them in the direction of extraction; natural capital approaches might in fact help present the hard evidence they need to address the unsustainability of the models they currently employ.

Even those who have dedicated their lives to preserving the natural world for its own sake now see the value of natural capital thinking. 'Economics is a discipline that shapes decisions of the utmost consequence, and so matters to us all,' says Sir David Attenborough of the Dasgupta Review. '[The report] at last puts biodiversity at its core and provides the compass that we urgently need. In doing so, it shows us how, by bringing economics and ecology together, we can help save the natural world at what may be the last minute – and in doing so, save ourselves.'[27]

Daily urged me not to lose sight of the forest for the trees. 'We've lost so much nature that adding it back almost anywhere is a massive benefit – that's the prize we need to keep our eyes on!'

It seemed that natural capital thinking was to her more pragmatic than ideological, borne of decades of disappointment with well-meaning public funders and private donors who had nevertheless fallen short of making the investments nature desperately needs. 'Philanthropy is never going to be enough to secure more than a tiny fraction of what we need. And we can see that nature reserves are just too small, too few, and too widely separated to add up. Morally, the course is really clear, actually, that we need more nature. And however we choose to convey that need and motivate people is legitimate, as long as we're being truthful about it.'

Daily's team at the NatCap was set up to convey that need with hard numbers. Housed at Stanford University, the project is a partnership between the Chinese Academy of Sciences, the University of Minnesota, and the Stockholm Resilience Centre, as well as The Nature Conservancy and World Wildlife Fund. The project's first goal was to develop clear intellectual frameworks (like ecosystem services) to think about natural capital, which it has now translated into an open-source software tool – InVEST – that brings data and models together to help decision-makers identify areas where natural capital investments can most benefit people and conservation.

Daily's role has taken her all over the world, from Belize and Colombia to China and Mongolia. She has spent weeks at a time on the road, making a compelling case for policymakers and businesses to wake up to the natural capital thinking she helped pioneer. Dozens across the world have taken her up on her offer to work with the NatCap team to integrate natural capital into their decision-making.

For all her work at the global level, Daily had always made her thinking on ecosystem services tangible by taking it back to the level of the individual.

She gestured to the oasis surrounding us. The pandemic had rooted her to the Stanford campus for nearly two years after a lifetime of constant travel, and the garden had become a pet project of sorts. 'Isn't it lovely?' she asked, rattling off facts from a series of studies from Finland to Oakland that have demonstrated the positive effect nature has on schoolchildren's development and mental health. 'These tiny elements show us that we don't always need to be going to Yellowstone or the Amazon, the places where we might like to go but are often impractical [to reach]... even just small doses of nature can be incredibly beneficial. We need to realise that we can all be stewards of that natural capital.'

Sir Partha shared a similar sentiment. 'My review was really written for the citizen,' he said, referring to the abridged version rather than the heftier full-length report. 'You've got to get the person down the pub to say no, we can no longer go on like this because I want my grandchildren to have the natural wealth I now know I take for granted.'

Businesses, governments and individuals face tricky trade-offs every day; what natural capital thinking does is help clarify the trade-offs between preserving and plundering nature. As we've seen, business cases for nature abound. As our leisurely lunch drew to a close, I invited Daily to reflect on a long career spent making these cases, and whether a tipping point was finally near.

'In the beginning, there were only a few iconic examples we could hold up, like New York City's watershed or Costa Rica's forest payments programme,' she told me. 'One thing that's really heartening and points to a leap is that we now have hundreds or thousands of such cases from across the world.'

As a parting thought, she pushed me to consider not only how we can replicate successful approaches from the past, but also how we can innovate to take natural capital thinking further and do it faster. 'I feel we need to rethink our systems of finance, accounting and policy, radically. We're not moving nearly quickly enough.'

As we'll see in the following chapter, technological and financial innovation is enabling the case for nature in ways that were unimaginable at the start of Daily's career. 'We need to start introducing more of the notion that we can transform societies through nature, and that there's a huge entrepreneurial opportunity for social innovation. We need to develop a system that invests in and drives regeneration everywhere. Our collective storytelling around nature needs to shift to that.'

As I drove home along Stanford's winding, palm-lined roads, I reflected on this place as the supposed heart of global technology and innovation. If places like this, and others across the world, could bring only a fraction of their immense creative talents to bear on the nature challenge, it felt as if the azure sky above me that day really was the limit.

Tech x Nature

One after the other, the giants made their way over to the watering hole, white tusks gleaming in the light. In the scrubby forest that surrounded them, giraffes and gazelle browsed through the trees; ostriches and secretary birds rooted through the ground; snake eagles and Nubian vultures circled overhead. As the midday heat grew, a languorous air seemed to descend on the wildlife and their human observers alike.

If elephants never forget, they certainly seemed to have forgiven the intrusion of a different sort of flyer. After all, just a few weeks ago, a state-of-the-art drone had buzzed all over this Kenyan landscape, armed with cameras, LiDAR and thermal sensors. The Harvard Animal Landscape Observatory, or HALO, had mapped every square inch of an ecosystem coming back from the brink.[1] I was now in Selenkay Conservancy, in Kilimanjaro's shadow, to see what technologies like this could do to make new cases for nature possible.

After all, this wasn't one of Kenya's many national parks and reserves, which are protected by law but cover just 8 per cent of this remarkable country. Instead, Selenkay lay off the beaten path that led to the far better-known Amboseli National Park on the Kenyan–Tanzanian border. This was Maasai rangeland; land that, along with other areas under indigenous stewardship, held the majority of Kenya's wildlife.

Two decades ago, Selenkay had paved the way for a community-led conservancy model that combined Maasai stewardship with low-impact tourism. Gamewatchers, a community-focused safari operator, had worked out a leasing model for 14,000 acres of land, set up a small tented camp that hosted no more than eighteen visitors at a time, and employed dozens of Maasai as guides, rangers and hotel staff. Three decades ago, Selenkay had been degraded by overgrazing and overtaken by invasive *Ipomea* vines. The community conservancy model had clearly worked, helping pay for restoration and turning it into a beacon of regeneration in a landscape that was increasingly under threat. Selenkay was now a haven for some of Kenya's largest elephants.

Walking into the community-run camp, I was immediately a fan. Porini Camp was effortlessly chic in some ways (colourful prints paired with earthy tones) but bare-bones in others (bucket showers, designed to conserve water in this semi-arid area). Gamewatchers had expanded the model to several other sites, more than tripling local incomes and building a faithful customer base of ecologically minded travellers. The pandemic hadn't been easy, but regulars had begun to return to the camps. Gamewatchers perfectly fit the mould of thoughtful ecotourism of the sort we've explored at length in this book.

But the Eselenkei Group Ranch, the 200,000 acres that surrounded Selenkay, was very much still subject to the pressures of a market economy. Kenya's rapid development – the shiny skyscrapers and well-paved highways – had come at the cost of traditionally managed land.

Kenya's Maasai had gradually seen their land transition from community stewardship to individual ownership; each member of Eselenkei, for instance, had been given a parcel of land on the order of fifty acres. In other parts of the country, drought and poverty had driven these new landowners to sell their land for as little as ten cows each (worth no more than a few thousand dollars). Driving south from Nairobi on a new, Chinese-built highway, it was clear to see how the new owners of these parcels had put up fences, walls, farms and factories where Acacia trees once stood sentinel over open savannah.

That mattered for East Africa's elephants, lions and wildebeest, which had evolved in vast, open landscapes, ranging widely and moving with the seasons. The great wildebeest migration of the Serengeti had once been mirrored all over Kenya and Tanzania. That was before vast, open ranges had been fragmented, connected only by corridors; corridors that had been progressively hemmed in and fenced off. The result had been a decline in migratory herbivore populations, and dramatic rise in human–wildlife conflict as elephants raided avocado farms and big cats picked off cattle.

In Eselenkei, the fences hadn't yet sprung up. But the legal 'subdivision' of the land had already taken place, aided by digital maps that gave each Maasai community member a shapefile of their plot of land in the place of physical markers and boundaries.

'Our community doesn't have a history of private land ownership, and I think there's a great challenge of the younger generation maybe wanting money now. Who can blame them? But if they sell their land for agriculture or something else, how will wildlife survive?' Ole Kasaine, a rising Maasai leader who went by Wilson, told me. 'Once they sell, the money soon evaporates, and people are left landless on their own land.'

Wilson had led a remarkable life. Born into a traditional Maasai community in Selenkay, he had walked the land for decades. As we moved through the varied landscape, he navigated by sight alone and was able to point out wildlife that my untrained eye could barely make out. I could see how deeply Wilson, who had trained as a spotter and guide and helped get the community conservancy off the ground, cared about his land and his people. He even knew each elephant, from the majestic tuskers to the calves that waddled around in the mud, by name.

'Nobody believed us when we said we could bring wildlife back and create good jobs for the community... that's why the creation of conservancies was paramount. And it still is. But we need to do a lot more, and we need to do it quickly, before the rest of our Maasai land is lost forever.'

Wilson was working with Viraj Sikand, an entrepreneur who had grown up in Kenya and cut his teeth working alongside anti-poaching patrols in the country's arid north. Viraj and Wilson's circles were filled with activists and conservationists: people who had campaigned to establish new wilderness areas, protect existing ones, and professionalise the country's wildlife agencies. I spoke to several of them; each cheered the tactical gains that Kenya had achieved, but each was convinced that progress on nature needed to accelerate to keep up with the pace of economic change.

They were now turning to technology to offer just such an acceleration. Sikand had partnered with Mohanjeet Brar of Gamewatchers, Maasai community leader Patita Nkamunu, veteran technology CEO Mark Tracy, and researchers at the Harvard Davies Lab who had developed the HALO drone, to set up a new venture called EarthAcre. 'The entire point of EarthAcre is to use technology to value each unique acre of indigenous-managed land,' Viraj told me. 'This includes the carbon stored on and under that land, but also the unique

The EarthAcre team with HALO drone used to survey
Selenkay. © EarthAcre, by permission.

biodiversity that exists on each acre. By mapping ecosystems
in unprecedented detail, we're hoping we can dramatically
reduce the time it takes to bring carbon and biodiversity-
related credits to market – and send benefits directly to the
people whose land we can then value and secure.'

Technology is by no means a cure-all. But in Selenkay, as in
several other pioneering sites across the world, economic cases
for nature – be they through ecotourism or ecosystem service
credits – are being enabled by dramatic advances in our ability
to measure and monitor, via eyes in the sky, sensors on the
ground and supercomputers in the cloud, in ways we simply
couldn't a decade ago.

But technology, of course, touches everything. As we saw in the chapter on nature-positive agriculture, technologies from bio-based fertilisers to precision fermentation are transforming the way we make our food. Clever biochemistry is allowing us to create ever-better replacements for products that degrade nature, from beef to palm oil. On carbon removal, technologies like biochar and bio-oil injection are able to take natural carbon from plants and lock it away in stable forms for thousands of years. Technologies like these, that produce tangible goods and services themselves, are already big business. Entire books could be, and have been, written on the ways in which these nuts-and-bolts technologies are transforming industries for the better.

However, in this chapter, my focus is on the technologies that *enable* business cases for nature. Many of these enablers are only just making their way out of laboratories and research projects, but they hold the potential to fundamentally transform the way we understand and value the natural world.

Technology of the enabling sort comes in many flavours. To make sense of it all, it might help to imagine a kind of **technology dashboard for the planet**, which could keep us abreast of all that's happening in the world's ecosystems and offer solutions to problems as they emerge.

* * *

For one, we'd certainly want eyes on the world's forests, fields, grasslands and oceans. In the past, the only way to do that was to send scientists out in the field, armed with field notebooks and transect maps. I've done this sort of painstaking work myself; fun as it can be the first couple of times, ground-based surveying is expensive and time-consuming. It is also prone to human error: I once got lost on a field survey in Wytham Woods, easily the world's best-studied patch of forest. One can imagine the challenges that come with surveying more uncharted ecosystems.

Technology is dramatically improving the situation. We can now observe the planet remotely and relatively cheaply, either from space with satellites or from the air by flying light aircraft or drones to map the landscape.

From their vantage points orbiting thousands of miles up, **satellites** can monitor vast areas of land and sea. As far back as the 1970s, the Landsat satellites launched by NASA and the US Geological Survey provided a rich trove of data for scientists looking to understand ecological systems. Like the camera on your phone, satellite cameras can detect light in the visible portion of the electromagnetic spectrum, allowing us to track whether a given piece of land is forest or field, and thus changes in deforestation and land use over time.[2]

But we can go even further, detecting wavelengths the human eye cannot see. Why is this sort of imaging important? Because the light that leaves reflect can reveal a great deal about the ecosystems they are in. For instance, satellites can now use 'multispectral' data to detect differences between types of green to identify which plant species are present in a forest and how productive they are.

LiDAR, or light detection and ranging, can take this precision even further by sending out laser beams, and measuring the way in which they bounce back to the source, to capture the three-dimensional structure of terrain and vegetation. LiDAR sensors are particularly useful for carbon measurement when airborne; the HALO drone that zipped across Selenkay could capture the structure of everything on the landscape. 'We now know, down to the centimetre level, exactly what the landscape looks like,' Viraj Sikand told me. 'That means we have a dataset for ecosystem restoration unlike any other – which enables us to model carbon and biodiversity like never before.' Remarkably, it took the drone just a couple of days to map thousands of acres; Sikand found that mounting the LiDAR sensor on a larger aircraft would enable EarthAcre to map thousands of square kilometres at a time, collecting high-precision data that could then be used to train satellite-based models of carbon and biodiversity. 'With that sort of scale, costs come down to cents per acre!' he said, contrasting this to the vast sums that can be spent on sending human auditors out to verify carbon projects.

Recent advances have taken LiDAR to space to provide global data from satellites, albeit at lower resolutions than

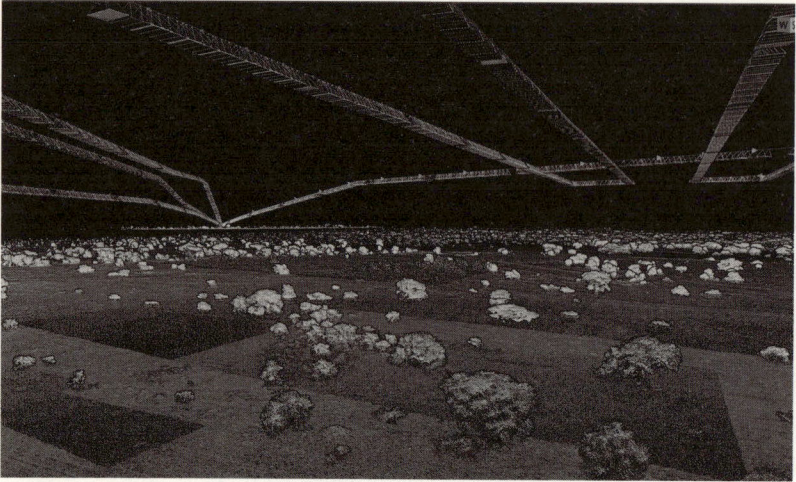

A LiDAR 'point-cloud' of Selenkay, with the drone's flight-path shown above. © EarthAcre, by permission.

airborne systems on drones or aircraft. NASA, as part of its Global Ecosystem Dynamics Investigation (GEDI), attached a LiDAR sensor to the international space station. Atticus Stovall, a scientist who helped develop the GEDI programme, offered his thoughts on what this meant for the future of monitoring ecosystems.

'LiDAR is basically like turning a forest – or really any environment – into a video game, instantly. It creates a totally virtual high-resolution reconstruction of the world,' he said. 'And GEDI is about taking that and upscaling it all the way to a global scale!'

Why is this useful? 'We're basically allowing lasers to hitch a ride on the space station [...] and using them to weigh the forests of the earth. Of course, these are predictions, rather than direct measurements [...] but with lasers, we've become really good at taking those predictions and translating them into a pretty confident measure of biomass and carbon and how it's changing over time.'

Satellites have been around for decades, but recent advances have now made them vastly more useful to scientists. Public agencies including NASA and the European Space Agencies have sent up ever-more-powerful instruments on new satellites, including an updated Landsat. A new breed of commercial satellite providers, such as Planet Labs, now provide high-frequency data from fleets of hundreds of smaller satellites. Rather than waiting weeks or months for a larger satellite to re-image the same location and detect changes, Planet Labs' satellites can provide daily or weekly data for farmers and conservation biologists alike.

'When we match LiDAR data to satellite imagery from Landsat, we have really high-resolution pictures of change on earth, combined with a measurement of carbon [...] we basically have everything we need to be able to know what we have where, how much it's changing, and what to do about it.'

Atticus emphasised that these advances go well beyond carbon. '[Biodiversity monitoring] is one of the exciting future directions for this work that links to nature as a whole – to understand habitats, habitat structures, and how species use those environments in three dimensions. That's why NASA's next decade is about pushing to understand all of the systems that govern life on earth.'

Satellites aren't only useful for imaging. GPS, the global positioning system that was initially developed for military use, provides an essential backbone for virtually all the mapping and tracking we do. But there are nature-specific mapping tools that have taken this further: since 2018, the ICARUS project has used an antenna on the International Space Station to enable the tracking of individual birds, mammals and even insects wearing tags weighing as little as four grams. On our hypothetical dashboard, using this kind of technology, we could assess in real time how animal populations are responding to changes in habitat, and act accordingly.

Encouragingly, these 'remote sensing' methods are moving beyond the academic research stage: new businesses are now building on these advances to create the business models that can help drive action on the ground. NCX, for instance, uses a large, satellite-derived dataset of North American forestry, developed with Microsoft's AI for Earth programme, to run the calculations that underpin its carbon market for foresters. NCX's model, which is based on deferring harvests so trees store more carbon before they are cut, would have been impossible without advances in satellite data and computational power.

Such advances have implications for other agricultural and working lands too. Companies have emerged to provide crop intelligence through an array of sensors, better measure carbon stocks above and below the ground, and track the resurgence of soil health as regenerative practices are adopted.

Working Trees, a company I was involved in founding while I was at Stanford, is now driving silvopasture adoption in the southeastern states of the US; it turned out that the LiDAR scanners and high-resolution cameras on iPhones, initially installed to improve virtual reality apps, could also provide a low-cost, decentralised way of tracking carbon storage in newly planted trees on pastureland. John Foye and Aakash Ahamed, who now co-lead the company, are on a mission to democratise access to carbon markets by using technology to allow every farmer to become a carbon farmer.

'Previously, you'd need a thousand acres to set up a reforest-ation project. Now, farmers of any size – whether they manage 100, 10 or even 1 acre – can enrol in our carbon programme. 'Without smartphone-based LiDAR, this simply wouldn't have been possible!' John told me as we caught up after one of his visits to Tennessee.

In parallel, open-access initiatives and innovative non-profits are turning transparency into a global public good. In mid-2022, Google and the World Resources Institute teamed up to launch Dynamic World, a freely accessible tool that, for the first time, offers near-real-time maps of global land cover.[3] A new platform from non-profit CTrees can now track the carbon stored in each individual tree across the world, offering greater transparency to the voluntary carbon markets. Such datasets once took months to put together, even if the raw data was available in real time; drawing on AI algorithms to speed up number-crunching, Dynamic World and CTrees can now shed light on both progress and backsliding, with near-real-time information deterring deforestation by allowing for rapid responses where it does occur.

Global Forest Watch (GFW), a non-profit, takes such datasets and draws out insights for conservationists, 'creating unprecedented transparency about what is happening in forests worldwide'. Why is this helpful? As GFW puts it, 'better information supports smarter decisions about how to manage and protect forests for current and future generations, and greater transparency helps the public hold governments and companies accountable for how their decisions impact forests'.[4]

As capable and potentially game-changing as these remote sensors are, our dashboard will always benefit from a dash of on-the-ground truth. 'A real bottleneck [problem] is collecting high-quality, ground-based data, to provide remote methods with a tangible connection to what we're measuring on the ground,' Atticus told me. 'A lot of my career has been spent in the field, hiking up crazy terrain and bushwhacking... as incredible as remote sensing is, there should be at least as much support given to in-field measurement.'

Here, too, technological advances are allowing us to understand ecosystems with a clarity that would have been unimaginable even a couple of decades ago.

Take **camera traps,** which revolutionised the detection of wildlife in hard-to-reach ecosystems, from the orangutans in the heart of Borneo to the snow leopards that stalk the mountaintops of Nepal. For decades, legacy camera traps – which are set off by any movement – would produce hundreds or thousands of false positives, mistaking any movement for an animal of interest. Human researchers would then have to retrieve cameras and parse through images manually to identify anything that might be useful: exactly as expensive and time consuming as you might imagine.

Today, camera traps are being paired with artificial intelligence models to automate this tedious task. Sentinel, a project from Conservation X Labs, retrofits existing cameras to run nifty algorithms on the images as they are captured. If a jaguar – or a poacher – is detected by Sentinel, it sends a notification to conservationists in near-real-time, allowing them to act far more quickly than they could have before.[5]

Cameras can be complemented by **bioacoustics** – a new set of tools that allows us to add digital ears to our tech-enabled eyes. While many large, charismatic animals like elephants or tigers can be easy to spot, birds and insects in particular can be hard to make out in dense forests. When I first trained as an ecologist, I was taught to identify bird species by learning their calls; as easy as it is for the naturally gifted, like Wilson, I could never quite get them all right. In any case, doing it the old-fashioned way involves trudging through the jungle for hours or days on end, which is educational for biologists-in-training, but not particularly scalable or efficient.

With bioacoustics, the basic premise is simple: microphones pick up audio across a wide range of frequencies – including those outside the range of human hearing – in order to identify both the *presence* or *absence* of certain species, and to get a sense of their *abundance* or population numbers. Beyond population data, animal calls can also provide a rich vein of information on animal behaviour: things like migration and mating patterns, and the presence of competitors and predators.

Project Dhvani – named for the Sanskrit word for sound – offers one example of how these rich datasets can serve the cause of ecosystem monitoring and management. Funded by Columbia University and National Geographic, among others, the Dhvani team is beginning to build and analyse an unprecedented dataset of sounds that could inform land management decisions in India.

'It's opened up an entire world for me!' Vijay Ramesh, one of the researchers on Project Dhvani, told me. 'In a tropical forest, you rarely *see* birds. Having analysed what we could *hear* through bioacoustics, I went, "Wow – there are actually a lot more species here than I imagined."' A game-changer has been the rapidly falling cost of recording devices: Dhvani's recorders only cost about $50 each.

Project Dhvani isn't just an exercise in scientific curiosity; researchers are focused on understanding whether, and to what extent, biodiversity recovers as forests are regrown in Central India and the Western Ghat range to the south. Vijay told me his bioacoustics data from land that had been reforested for over twenty years yielded some surprising results. 'The birds had mostly come back... but higher frequencies between 12,000 to 24,000Hz, the ones where insects are active, were just empty. It was basically empty across every single restored and degraded forest site.' The reasons for this are still being worked out, but through bioacoustics the team discovered an important blind spot in the tracking of ecosystem recovery.

Still, Dhvani is running into the limits of the algorithms that speed the processing of recordings. It turns out that many of the computational models developed to date were focused on temperate regions of North America and Europe, and trained on datasets from regions where one might hear a single bird call every few seconds. 'In the tropical forests of India, you have a cacophony of birds, so the models are actually performing fairly poorly here,' Vijay told me. The Dhvani team is beginning to build their own neural network from scratch, manually tagging files so the machine-learning models can adapt to a noisier ecosystem.

If eyes in the sky and ears on the ground are valuable and ever-improving sources of intelligence for our planetary dashboard, technology is now advancing to the point where even the rarest plants, animals, microbes and fungi are unable to slip our monitoring nets.

It turns out that virtually everything – from the smallest bacterium swimming about in a pond, to a gazelle that may have taken a gulp of water before dashing off into the scrub, to a Canada lynx padding through the snow – sheds tiny fragments of DNA. This environmental DNA, called **eDNA**, can now be amplified and analysed against a database – a technique known as metabarcoding – to reveal the hidden inhabitants of ecosystems and the ways in which they change over time.

eDNA can be extracted from water bodies or the soil, but it can even be found floating around in the air. One study in Copenhagen Zoo detected forty-nine species of vertebrates just from sucking eDNA out of the air, including rhinos, giraffes, elephants and even a guppy that lived in a pond in the rainforest house.[6]

As with several of the applications we've explored here, the plummeting cost of the underlying technology has played a huge part in making commercial eDNA sequencing possible. At the turn of the twenty-first century, sequencing a single human genome cost over $100 million; in 2022, that had fallen to under $500, vastly outpacing the Moore's Law curve that has roughly tracked the rise of cheap and plentiful computing power.[7] A commercial eDNA sample now costs just a couple of hundred dollars, shipping included: a drop in the bucket for conservation projects accustomed to enormous monitoring costs.

No wonder then that entire businesses are being built on this novel enabler. NatureMetrics, one such start-up, has supported hundreds of commercial eDNA projects that run the gamut from manatee detection in Peru for the WWF, to fish stock analysis in the Thames, to ensuring that developers in England are able to carry out conservation banking for the Great Crested Newt. In each of these cases, eDNA enabled a business case for conservation far more cheaply and quickly than human monitors could. Katie Critchlow, one of the co-founders of NatureMetrics, described how companies were making the most of their tech-enabled offering.

'The exciting thing is that our more progressive clients are beginning to go far beyond ticking boxes. Because they get such a depth of data from the DNA, they're finding species, rare and threatened and protected species, they never knew were there. We've got a nice example of one of our mining clients who found a rare otter on their site. And they got really excited by that, [to the extent] that they worked with the farmers all around the mining site to put in place a management plan for that species,' she said.

But it went beyond feel-good stories. With talk of nature-related risks and disclosures becoming commonplace in large companies, Katie explained how NatureMetrics was beginning to expand its range of services. 'We now add in a whole new layer of analysis and decision-support for our clients that enables them to talk about biodiversity in the boardroom. That includes simple, clear visualisations of change that let them determine if biodiversity is getting better or worse.

'Because biodiversity data has been so poorly delivered to date, you're at the point of the curve where more data leads to action very quickly and easily. I know that having data isn't the be all and end all. But what gets measured gets managed, and we're only just beginning to see the effects of being able to serve that data up to buyers who are viewing it not only through a lens of regulatory compliance.'

Beyond progressive companies looking to build nature-positive supply chains, it seemed to us both that eDNA (and other conservation tech) could also shine a spotlight on inadequate or fraudulent activity in carbon markets, ecotourism, regenerative agriculture and the like. 'The game-changer was when people started being able to monitor methane emissions from the sky,' Katie said. 'Because it didn't matter what Shell reported on its methane emissions: we *know* what they are. And [it's] similar with eDNA.'

I decided to try it out for myself. Katie's team shipped me a pair of soil sample kits, and I went eDNA hunting on Windy Hill, a nature preserve with panoramic views of the San Francisco Bay Area. All I needed was to scoop some soil into a little plastic pot, add a preservative buffer, and ship it to the lab to be analysed.

I held on to the second kit for a while, wondering what to do with it: biosecurity regulations make it tricky to take samples in some countries, and paperwork has never been my strong suit. In the end, I chose to go back to the beautiful

Taking eDNA samples in Gretchen Daily's Palo Alto garden.

garden where I had had lunch with Gretchen Daily to see what eDNA data I might collect there.

A few weeks later, the results were in. The NatureMetrics team had run three sets of analyses on the bacterial, fungal and faunal (animal) eDNA they found in my samples, identifying hundreds of taxa (groups of species) for each. The results threw up everything from white pot worms to deer truffles, several types of spider, and even a plant parasite known to cause powdery mildew. I received a tree-of-life chart comparing the Windy Hill site with Gretchen's garden, each showing a visibly different community of microbes and critters. All this, from two little scoops of soil.

While my far-fetched hopes that a lynx might show up in the soil samples were dashed, the science team at NatureMetrics emphasised that the bigger picture was key. 'We generally focus less on species lists generated by individual samples [and instead] collect multiple samples across a habitat to create a soil community fingerprint. This can then be used to compare different habitats or land management practices, or to track habitat restoration success over time.'

eDNA only scratches the surface of the mind-boggling complexity of the ecological systems that surround us. 'The fact that we know so little should mean we keep as much of it intact as possible!' Katie said. 'The basic thing you learn as an ecologist is that the more of the Jenga blocks you take out, the more the tower is likely to fall over.' Perhaps, after all, the

Cenococcum geophilum fungus they found in my samples was just as important as a more charismatic cat.

One of the biggest financial stories in recent years, for better or for worse, has been the rise of **web3**, an umbrella term for the decentralised, blockchain-based technologies that promised to revolutionise everything from finance to the fabric of society itself. In 2021, record levels of venture capital (VC) flowed into web3 start-ups: nearly $18 billion, by one count, compared to the puny $0.2 billion in VC dollars invested in reforestation and ecosystem restoration ventures in the two years to April 2022.[8,9] To me, the comparison is stark and rather depressing, even if the web3 bubble subsequently deflated spectacularly in 2022. Despite the paucity of genuine applications for environmental or ecological action so far, a ray of hope comes in the form of the environmental concern that has begun to percolate these web3 circles – circles that are worth understanding in case they do come up with useful cases for nature in the years ahead.

While I won't attempt to explain the tangle of web3 terms in any great depth, a handful of key ones can help you navigate this maze. First, there is the **blockchain** - a distributed digital ledger that, much like an accountant's notebook, allows users to record transactions. Only here, no single accountant is in control. The blockchain lives on a network, and the inherent design makes it impossible to manipulate by any single entity.

As a single source of truth, the blockchain is meant to enable a number of applications that rely on trust. You might recognise blockchains for the **cryptocurrencies,** like Bitcoin, that they have enabled – tokens, based on an underlying scarcity, that have seen fortunes made and lost overnight.

A related term is a **smart contract,** a blockchain-enabled programme that automatically kicks in, without any intermediary enforcing the rules, when certain conditions are met.

The two taken together have enabled the creation of decentralised autonomous organisations, or **DAOs**, which to me seem like leaderless cooperatives built for the digital age. Founded on smart contracts, DAOs are governed by the votes of the members that constitute them; any change to the activities of the DAO, or a decision to disband it, can be triggered by any member and voted on by everyone else.

Finally, there are non-fungible tokens, or **NFTs**. Enabled by those public, unchangeable ledgers, NFTs function as certificates of ownership and authenticity for digital assets. NFTs enable users to own artificially scarce digital items such as unique works of art, objects in online games, or exclusive recordings of musicians. While the legal implications are still unclear, NFTs can also represent physical assets, such as a parcel of land. Many of these technologies are beginning to be used in the 'metaverse': a dressed-up term for cyberspace, as opposed to the physical universe we inhabit. Enthusiasts on the cutting edge may talk of DAOs and NFTs, but the hype cycle will doubtless have moved on further by the time these words make it into print.

Plenty has been written about web3, including about the tremendous impact that Bitcoin 'mining', which involves setting computers to process Bitcoin code and generate new coins in return, can have on carbon emissions. With a carbon footprint the size of New Zealand's, the emissions impact of Bitcoin is an important question, although improvements are possible: in 2022, technical changes dramatically slashed the emissions of Bitcoin's main competitor, Ethereum. For this story, what matters is whether so-called web3 technologies can enable us to do real things that move the needle on our all-too-real planetary challenges. In my scan of the landscape, three broad applications of web3 appear to be taking hold.

First, distributed ledgers are being explored for their potential to build trust and verifiability into carbon and ecosystem service markets. As things stand, many carbon trades are 'over the counter', sold between buyers and sellers without the market infrastructure that exists for, say, stocks. A Bloomberg terminal is a fantastic source of live, real-time data on stock price movements and volumes; the same cannot yet be said to exist for these nascent markets. While capital markets show how trust certainly can be built into systems without web3, decentralised ledgers are intended to solve the same challenge without reconstructing the many systems that make the traditional financial world go round.

Regen Network, an early mover in the web3 space, launched one such carbon and ecosystem ledger in 2022; the Regen Ledger, it said, was 'built to serve as Earth's public registry of ecological claims and assets'. Legacy banks have also jumped aboard the crypto train. Carbonplace, a new initiative launched by seven large banks including UBS and Standard Chartered, aims to create the 'settlement infrastructure' of choice for carbon markets and exchanges.

While decentralised ledgers claim to bring radical transparency to carbon markets, a new breed of DAOs is taking on a different challenge: that of expanding markets for carbon reduction and removal, including through nature-based methods. Much of the interest in DAOs comes from a typically bewildering set of rules they adopt, referred to as 'tokenomics', that they hope can create wealth for members. They can often resemble Ponzi schemes, with prices going up as more buyers enter the system.

In some cases, there is no base value for their tokens beyond artificial scarcity. In many carbon-focused DAOs, however, tokens are backed by carbon credits, which themselves fluctuate in value. I won't attempt to explain the dynamics of these tokenomics systems – including the wild price swings that can come from waves of interest as they ebb and flow. As far as get-rich-quick schemes go, DAOs create winners and losers; the question for us is whether DAOs can fundamentally increase demand for new carbon removal and help to restore nature in the process.

In the chapter on carbon markets, we learnt that not all carbon credits are created equal. Some DAOs, such as the Eden DAO, have set a high bar on what credits they will accept and partnered with Patch, a reputable marketplace that aggregates what are generally considered high-quality credits. More liquidity into high-quality carbon credits does, to my mind, seem worthwhile. But in many cases, DAOs have ended up actively harming the integrity of the carbon markets they hope to improve.

The saga of the Klima DAO, and the Toucan protocol it relies on, proved how well-intentioned applications of web3 can have unintended consequences. Explicitly set up to sweep the floor of cheap, low-quality credits and drive up carbon credit prices so that new projects become more profitable, the Klima–Toucan combination – which was far bigger than Eden – unwittingly ended up driving funding to old, worthless carbon credits. These included supposedly 'additional credits' that turned out to channel money to profitable renewable energy projects that had already been built, which created essentially no new climate benefit, and which real buyers would never have funded.

'Toucan appears to be generating entirely new demand for long-neglected credits that have experienced little or no demand in recent years,' CarbonPlan reports. 'We found that about 28 per cent of Toucan-bridged credits (representing 6.0 million tonnes of CO_2-equivalent) come from what we call zombie projects,' they wrote, referring to low-quality projects that had found no buyers on the open market for years before Toucan and Klima came along. 'In the end, a blockchain-based carbon offset strategy is only as good as the credits on which it is founded. When organisations like Toucan or KlimaDAO outsource quality control to the carbon offset registries, they risk not only mirroring the problems in today's voluntary markets [...] they also risk becoming the dumping ground for credits that have already been weeded out by more conscientious buyers.'[10]

DAOs and their arcane rules stand in contrast to the simpler logic that underlies NFTs: buyers pay to own something, typically intangible but sometimes physical, and can prove their ownership with a unique token. Many use NFTs purely to speculate, buying NFTs of cartoon apes and first-of-a-kind tweets in the hope that they can sell them on at a higher price; by mid-2022, those frothy markets had already begun to recede. Strip away dreams of riches and what NFTs offer, in some cases, is the chance to contribute to ecosystem restoration and receive a unique memento in return.

I spoke to Neal Spackman, who works with local and indigenous communities across the planet to help revive traditional farming and aquaculture practices and restore degraded coastal land. But Neal also launched an NFT project, 100 Million Mangroves, and I wanted to know what had led a committed natural capital entrepreneur to dabble in web3.

'I was somewhat aware of NFTs. But they began exploding in the summer of 2021, and we had this opportunity. We had a brilliant artist, Saiful Haque, and I asked him if we could do an NFT project and direct 100 per cent of the funds to mangrove restoration. That's how we got started,' Neal told me. Each donor received a unique work of art in exchange for their contribution to the project.

It seemed to me that the mangrove NFTs were simply adding a web3 twist to philanthropic crowdsourcing. 'One of the main criticisms of NFTs is that you don't own the real thing, right? Anyone can copy that, and anyone can take the data. But in our case, we don't want you to buy the birds, and the lizards and the fish that are increasing in abundance. What you can have is ownership of an NFT that reflects the data,' he said. 'In turn, you get to say look, I've purchased this thing, that means I'm contributing to an increase in biodiversity, I am providing a venue for life on this planet to increase. That's an [NFT-enabled] biodiversity credit.'

Only 8 per cent of global charitable giving goes to environmental causes; perhaps the one-of-a-kind storytelling that forms part of the appeal of these tokens can help unlock an entirely new pool of donors for restoration projects.[11] Another project, Moss, is taking this NFT-based funding approach and applying it to physical land parcels in the Amazon, each the size of a football field, that are at risk of deforestation.[12]

While I remain doubtful that these projects have applicability beyond something that looks on the face of it rather like philanthropy, Neal raised the prospect of more applications as the space matures, including ones linked to cryptocurrencies and the other building blocks of web3. 'I don't know that we're monetizing ecology as much as we are ecologising money. That gets to the bigger dreams of the web3 world, the idea that we can create currencies that are backed by natural capital, where there's some reflection of soil and ecology and water, or ocean health, reflected in a currency. That's a big dream. I don't know if that dream is possible. But I do know that I can create a product today that can help me put more money towards funding biodiversity than we have now.' That, I could get behind.

As we explore the many ways in which the business case for nature can be enabled by technology, our planetary dashboard is really beginning to come together. We can now monitor nature more precisely and cheaply than at any point in human history. Precision is important because it brings trust into markets that have up to now often lacked it, and therefore failed to scale. In the past, making the economic case for nature meant taking grand leaps of faith that carbon really was being stored, or that biodiversity really was bouncing back. Technology is making those leaps smaller by the year, so that we can be surer of getting what we pay for when we invest in nature.

The cost-cutting powers of technology are also important. In the past, restoration budgets would be consumed by immense overheads. Now, the rapidly falling costs of technology-enabled monitoring are transformative to project economics, allowing developers to allocate more of the benefits of carbon storage, ecotourism or agriculture projects to direct action – action that ultimately restores ecosystems and funnels money to the communities that need it.

Increasingly, actors in these spaces are aware that bringing several of these tools together can add up to more than the sum of their parts. In Kenya, EarthAcre is already planning to deploy bioacoustics in addition to satellite- and drone-based LiDAR data. 'Our hope is to create the most comprehensive set of biodiversity metrics out there, and we can't do that credibly without integrating multiple sources of data,' Viraj told me as we bounced down the rutted dirt track that led out of Selenkay.

'With EarthAcre, the hope is that buyers of carbon or biodiversity credits will reward us for being able to tell them a credible story of how biodiversity is returning to Maasai-managed land.' Viraj added that the team was looking into photos, videos and even NFTs as means to connect buyers to the unique attributes of each acre they were helping to restore.

Sarika Khanwilkar of Dhvani echoed the value of using technology to forge connections with far-away wildernesses. 'What excites me about acoustics is its use as a way to engage people with nature and get them excited about it. The sounds of nature are disappearing, and we can use [bioacoustics] to foster people's deep-seated curiosity about biodiversity.' Having been raised on Sir David Attenborough's documentaries, we all know how earlier advances in visual media turned generations of city-dwellers and suburbanites into ardent nature lovers. Perhaps new frontiers are within reach.

Wilson concurred, gazing out of the windows of the jeep as we passed herds of wildebeest basking in the sun. This was, after all, his land. Land that had been in Maasai hands for generations; land that had raised him, and that he was now helping secure for generations to come. He related stories about his childhood; about his father's brushes with rhinoceroses and lions; about the aspirations he had for places like Kenya.

For all the exciting market-making and monitoring advances that technology is enabling, often overlooked is the ability to record and disseminate the impact of stories like Wilson's in near-real-time; stories of hope, change and revival that are so important if we are to build momentum on the biodiversity crisis. The ways in which technology can help us forge and maintain our connections with the Earth might be just as worthwhile as the construction of a technological dashboard of planetary proportions.

Fighting Fire with Finance

The twisting drive had taken us high up into the American Sierra Nevada mountains. As we rounded the corner, a breathtaking view came into sight: an enormous, stunningly clear body of water encircled by hillsides covered in pine forest. It wasn't hard to see why Lake Tahoe, one of the world's largest and deepest mountain lakes, is a nature-lover's paradise, thronged in turn by hikers and paddleboarders in the summer, and skiers and snowboarders in the winter.

Tahoe, and the myriad other lakes and rivers that make up this iconic landscape, would not exist without its richly forested watershed, the traditional heartland of the Washo Tribe. California's gold rush in the late 1800s brought white settlers and a pattern of indigenous exclusion and erasure that is, by now, depressingly familiar. As railroads brought development and extraction to the Sierra Nevada, first-wave conservationists, for all their grave shortcomings, began to take note.

In 1905, Theodore Roosevelt created the Yuba Forest Preserve and expanded the existing Tahoe Forest Preserve; a year later, the two preserves were combined to form the Tahoe National Forest, which remains a federally protected area to this day.

If enshrining Tahoe's conservation in law had been enough, there wouldn't be much of a story to tell. It so happened that while federal protection did slash commercial logging, federal authorities also embarked on a long programme of fire suppression – a programme that yielded decades of relative calm, followed by fiery storm. Fuelled by woody debris in unnaturally dense forests, and exacerbated by historic droughts and careless holidaymakers, wildfires in the Sierras now burn with a terrifying intensity on an almost-yearly basis.

The authorities are increasingly clear-eyed about what needs to be done: forests must be thinned, dead wood cleared, and natural meadows and aspen stands restored so that easy-burning conifers no longer encroach on these open spaces. In short, bringing fire resilience to Tahoe means 'restoring' a landscape that looks, to the untrained eye, pleasantly forested, but is in reality dangerously overgrown and desperately in need of a return to its patchier primaeval state.

All of that costs money, which brings us to the eternal question that we've explored throughout this book: who will pay? The US Forest Service (USFS) is chronically underfunded, and more and more of its budget must be spent fighting fires rather than preventing them. In 1995, the USFS devoted 16 per cent of its budget to firefighting; a decade later, that figure had soared to over 50 per cent, and has continued to rise ever since.[1, 2] But there are others – from public water agencies to insurers – who would benefit financially from proactively tackling the causes of wildfires. These institutions *would* pay, if they *could*: what was needed was a dash of financial innovation.

That's where Zach Knight and the team at Blue Forest Conservation came in. A non-profit set up to 'fight fire with finance', their **Forest Resilience Bond** (FRB) – a financial instrument designed to draw in private capital to complement public and philanthropic money – had just been successfully piloted in the Tahoe National Forest. Now, Zach and the team are hoping to take this financial creativity to the rest of the Western United States.

The statistics on investment in nature are clear: there simply isn't enough of it happening. The Paulson Institute estimated that the world currently spends $124–143 billion on conservation of all sorts, across government spending, philanthropy, offsets and sustainable supply chains. That figure is dwarfed by the harmful subsidies the world's governments carve out for agriculture, forestry and fishing, totalling over half a trillion dollars. The Institute estimated that the 'biodiversity financing gap', the amount the world needs to rustle up by 2030 to add to the meagre amount it currently spends to tackle the many crises in the natural world, is at least $600 billion, and perhaps as high as $820 billion.[3]

Private and public investors have been waking up to this need. New funds are being set up to invest in natural carbon projects, nature-positive supply chains, climate-tech start-ups and the like. But as important as it is to push up aggregate funding into nature, this is not a chapter on the need for more investment. That case has been compellingly made elsewhere.

Instead, in this chapter I want to explore the clever ways in which we can put that money to use, highlighting how actors from across sectors are engaging in financial innovation in service of natural capital.

Blue Forest's model aims to solve a problem that all public lands face: the costs of restoration are all borne up-front, while the benefits are spread out over many years. Once the Forest Service had identified areas to restore and thin, Blue Forest went out to find what they called beneficiaries – other entities who might have a financial interest in improving forest health.

One of these entities was the Yuba Agency, which manages the Yuba watershed. Willie Whittlesey, who helped forge Yuba's FRB project, said the cost-benefit calculations that Blue Forest presented to them 'simply made business sense. It costs us about a million dollars every ten years to remove woody debris, and it costs us $4 million to remove sediments. And that's in a forest that hasn't burned. If you layer on a catastrophic wildfire, those costs are going to go up tenfold. We'd rather pay to avoid that!' He added that there were harder-to-quantify benefits to water quality and quantity that made the case even stronger.

In parallel, Blue Forest lined up investors - entities who were able to the provide money required up-front to carry out restoration, and who could then be paid back over time, with interest, as the benefits accrued to the beneficiaries. By turning a daunting restoration project into a series of predictable, expected cash flows from beneficiaries, such as Cal Fire and Yuba, Blue Forest had made the trees of Tahoe investable.

One such investor was CSAA, an insurance agency based in California that naturally had an interest in the state's growing wildfire problem. 'Think of us as a financial first responder,' Jeff Huebner, CSAA's Chief Risk Officer, told me. 'We come in more or less at the same time as firefighting happens, and we're there after the fact to help people rebuild. And we recognised that [...] growing wildfires were becoming an existential threat to us. So we asked ourselves – should we just be a financial first responder and respond after the fact? Or do we go upstream? How might we make an investment that makes an appropriate financial return, and bring multiple returns from an environmental and social perspective?'

And so, the first FRB was born. Borrowing from a playbook that is by now standard for grey infrastructure projects, but hadn't yet been tried for natural systems, the Blue Forest model channelled investor money to pay for restoration and got beneficiaries like Yuba and the Forest Service to return that capital gradually over time as the forest's health improved.

Core to the FRB's success was the clever partnership it had forged between investors and beneficiaries, and the supporting coalition of nine federal, state, tribal and NGO stakeholders who had come together to form the North Yuba Forest Partnership in 2019. Zach Knight, Blue Forest's co-founder and CEO, explained how and why the public and private worlds had been brought together in this way.

'In the policy world, we talk about the need for *funding* nature. When we are in the [private sector] world, we talk about *financing* things. These words are used interchangeably but they mean different things.

'And we do both at Blue Forest, which is very odd, right? What we do is line up a series of different *fundings* coming from the federal, state and ultimately local government, and then *finance* against that in the form of a public–private partnership.' The key was working out how to structure those cash flows. 'It's all about finding ways to smooth [cash flows]

A forester in Blue
Forest's project area.
© Blue Forest, by permission.

a little bit each year, to make everything we're doing more predictable and efficient,' Knight said.

With its pilot scheme, Blue Forest had set out to answer three questions: 'Can these entities enter into these types of contracts? Can you monitor the benefits to get them to do that? And will investors accept all this?' The answer to all three, it turned out, was a resounding yes. With a successful first pilot under its belt, the Yuba Water Agency was keen to expand the programme to all 300,000 acres they managed. Nationally, the USFS forged an agreement to begin expanding the FRB across six other states, and to see if similar financial structures could help with post-fire-restoration as well as proactive management. 'Collaborative partnerships and financial mechanisms that leverage public and private capital other than Forest Service appropriations [budget allocations] are key strategies in the 10-Year Wildfire Crisis Strategy,' says Nathalie Woolworth of the Forest Service; they lay the groundwork for efforts like Blue Forest's to take root.

'We've come to the point now with the Forest Service where they say, "we see this work is so valuable, we'd like to also invest in it." Now, we have the federal government, through two different programs, committing $55 million to invest in this area over the next ten years. So it's an absolutely massive investment,' Zach Knight said excitedly. He acknowledged that more work needed to be done to convince investors to scale up their commitments, but asserted that the first FRB had been a valuable proof point 'to have the belief that this can be done at the $10-million scale and then eventually the $100-million scale'.

Willie seemed up for the challenge. 'We've got to get working on forest restoration at a pace and scale that we haven't ever seen before. This is the right thing to do. Getting our forests, especially in the West [of the United States], in the condition they were in prior to the 1850s is the target. That's what's going to create a landscape that is actually resilient to wildfire and climate change.'

In basic terms, financial innovations for nature often take the structures and tools that make traditional high finance go, and tweak them so they can channel money into our living planet instead. Finance innovators are finding ways to retool instruments including performance-linked bonds and insurance, credit ratings, and common stock ownership to serve nature-positive ends. Let's explore some of the ways in which financial innovation is enabling the other cases for nature.

Insurance, that everyday purchase we use to protect our investments in property, cars or holidays, is a product that simply transfers risk away from the individual towards a pooled fund that can pay out to the unlucky few in bad times in exchange for a relatively modest annual payment. Why not do the same for environmental assets and the people who rely on them?

The Mesoamerican Reef (MAR), the second largest barrier reef in the world, has become a test bed for exactly this. A tremendously biodiverse strip running along the Caribbean coasts of Mexico, Belize, Guatemala and Honduras, the reef provides coastal protection, reduces beach erosion, acts as a fish nursery, and supports the Riviera Maya tourism hub which generates $10 billion annually. Healthy reefs also act as the first line of defence against hurricanes and storms, reducing wave energy by up to 97 per cent.[4]

In 2019, Mexico's Quintana Roo state government decided to invest in protecting this valuable natural asset, taking out an insurance policy with global reinsurance giant Swiss Re, with help from the Nature Conservancy. The devil was in the detail: once a storm sweeps through and damages a reef, time is of the essence. If funds are available to rapidly assess damage and begin replanting, reefs stand a better chance of recovering before the next storm. So the insurance policy was designed as a 'parametric' one, which pays out automatically when a publicly verifiable metric is breached, rather than waiting for assessors to work methodically, as they might do after a car crash, and assign a dollar cost to the damages. In this case, a Category 3 hurricane – over 100 knots, independently measured by the National Hurricane Centre – was set as the threshold to trigger the payout.

The timing was fortuitous. In 2020, Hurricane Delta hit, and the policy paid out $850,000 virtually immediately to fund repairs along the coast. Having seen the benefits of the scheme, the MAR Fund, a non-profit comprised of conservation funds in each country of the MAR region, is taking out a second policy to cover a far larger section of the reef, extending this insurance protection to parts of Guatemala, Belize and Honduras. In parallel, the fund also plans to support an emergency response brigade of divers who can zip in and begin restoration as soon as the insurance policy pays out.[5]

Reefs are simply the most charismatic of coastal systems; systems like mangroves and seagrass can offer even greater flood protection benefits to communities. The Nature Conservancy released a report in December 2020 investigating the feasibility of rolling out this model to more reefs and other habitats.[6]

The World Bank, for its part, has laid out a sweeping vision for the role of the insurance industry in addressing the biodiversity crisis. In its 2022 report, *Insuring Nature's Survival*, the Bank outlines the ways in which insurers can help protect natural assets and facilitate greater investment, calling biodiversity loss 'an increasingly important source of risk and opportunity for the insurance sector'.[7] Still, the idea of insuring nature remains, for now, niche at best.

Nephila, a specialist catastrophe and weather-risk insurer, has managed to build an entire business on helping businesses and governments cope with the threats that extreme weather events and climate change pose to their assets, a market that once seemed unlikely to get off the ground.

Barney Schauble, chairman of Nephila, told me there were three key questions all insurers had to answer when setting up a new insurance scheme: the accuracy of risk prediction, how much to charge, and how large the market could be over time. 'The final one is key. If one person has a $5 million problem, it's not that interesting [...] but if many more have the same problem, and it could be a billion-dollar market, that's when you can construct a portfolio of risk.'

He agreed that pilot projects like the one in Quintana Roo held promise but asserted that more was needed to begin scaling up demand for nature insurance. 'The pilot projects can prove that there's a way to execute something. But what you really need [...] is some pressure to say, let's make this consistent. And right now, for most of these countries, companies, and individuals, there isn't really external pressure to hedge against losses.'

Things could change rapidly if policymakers were able to stimulate such demand, he said, pointing to India's successful rollout of crop insurance to its vast smallholder agriculture sector. 'Five or six years ago, the government decided that simply being the backstop for farmers having a poor agricultural season wasn't a long-term answer. So they encouraged the development of local crop insurance providers. Even though they're highly subsidised and a lot of the premium is paid by the government, the idea was to at least put into place a framework where you start to have a private marketplace. Now you have a big market. And, when things go bad, there's also some capital coming from outside India into that market to support when there's too little rain or too much rain. Eventually, you can start to remove the subsidy. But now there's a whole ecosystem in place of agents and companies and reinsurance companies.'

As we spoke, it became clear to me that demand for insurance could come from all quarters: carbon offset developers might purchase insurance against wildfires; ecotourism and agricultural businesses might do the same for droughts or storms; and cities might wake up to the fact of their financial interest in hedging against losses of coastal ecosystems.

'What gives me hope is that there are a lot of smart people and a lot of capital mobilised to try to change the shape of decision-making. Now it's really just a question of speed. You know, it's 2022… not 2012 or 1985 when people were just starting to think about this. So it's really a question of, can we galvanise that capital rapidly enough?'

Insurers can certainly help manage downside risk, but proactive investment is often the first line of defence. Some organisations are taking **outcome-based financing**, much like Blue Forest is pioneering in North America, and applying it to fund a broader set of biodiversity interventions.

In March 2022, the first ever wildlife conservation bond was launched by the World Bank and its partners. Dubbed a 'rhino bond', this five-year, $150 million, outcome-based financial structure channels investments to conserve black rhino populations in two national parks in South Africa. Investors don't receive an annual coupon payment; instead, if conservation efforts are successful, they receive a performance fee, paid for as a grant by the Global Environment Facility, in addition to the money they invested. Why was this interesting to investors? Because, in a high-rhino-growth scenario of 4 per cent per year, they could get a return greater than the rate on standard World Bank bonds; in a medium scenario, they'd do about as well as they would have otherwise, while they would get their principal back but accept lower returns if rhino populations did poorly.[8]

Structuring it so investors could take a risk on rhino growth in exchange for potentially higher returns meant private investors were able to magnify the impact of scarce donor money. In effect, donors could be sure that they were only paying out (to private investors, who fronted the cash) when conservation outcomes were met. For its part, South Africa's government was able to finance rhino conservation in two ecologically important protected areas, and provide community livelihoods in these areas, without adding to its sizable stock of sovereign debt.

Another innovation has been in the area of **debt-for-nature swaps**, which offer debt forgiveness in exchange for guarantees on environmental outcomes. The idea was first piloted in the Seychelles in 2018, when creditors came to accept that the heavily indebted country was unlikely to pay off all of its debts. In return for debt relief, the Seychelles agreed to channel some of the savings into marine conservation and create policies that protected 30 per cent of its seas.

In the case of the Seychelles, the amount of debt forgiven was small, on the order of a few million dollars, but, in 2022, Belize took this one step further. The government, working with the Nature Conservancy and other partners, executed a debt-for-nature swap that bought back over half a billion dollars of commercial debt that had been trading at 55 cents on the dollar (implying that bondholders had little faith in Belize's ability to repay the debt). The new debt was structured as a 'blue bond' – with the American Development Finance Corporation throwing political-risk insurance into the mix.[9]

In a stroke, Belize's debt went from unsustainable to investment-grade, and the transaction slashed the country's overall debt burden by 9 per cent of GDP. Using part of the savings, Belize agreed to spend $180 million on marine conservation over the next twenty years. I have been fortunate to see for myself the beauty of Belize's underwater treasures and the majesty of the Great Blue Hole, the unique giant marine sinkhole that lies within in its barrier reef system. Seeing this small country take such a large stride towards conserving them fills me with hope.

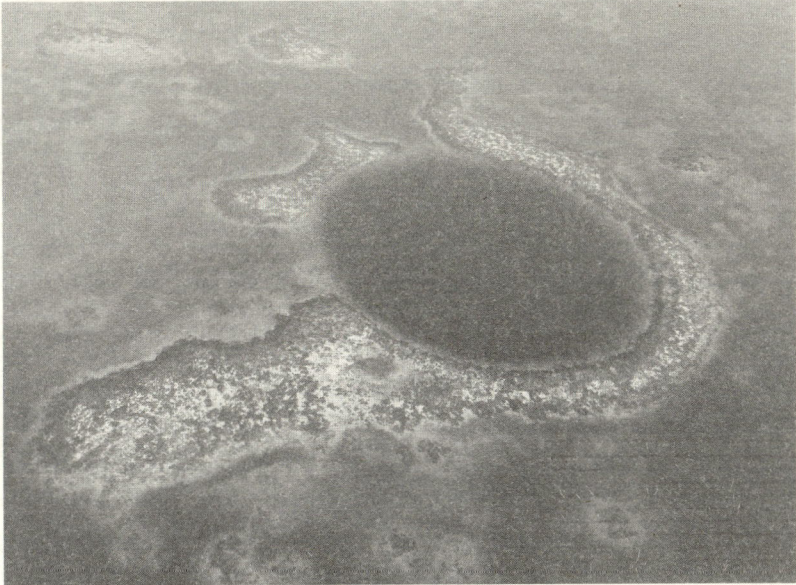

The Belize Blue Hole, part of the barrier reef ecosystem that will now receive greater funding as a result of the deal.

Indeed, both transactions turned out to be a triple win: for the countries that cut their unsustainable debt, for the creditors who had been unlikely to be repaid in any case, and for the marine ecosystems that now have stable, long-term sources of conservation funding. As biodiversity-rich developing countries struggle to service their debts in the face of post-Covid market turmoil, more such deals are in the offing.

Samantha Power, a nature finance consultant who has worked for the World Bank, spoke of the prospect of expanding this approach to other areas. 'Countries like Gabon and Colombia, for instance, have vast, intact rainforests that provide ecosystem services, including carbon sequestration and water cycling, across regions and the globe. These eco-system services are incredibly important for economies and societies and are becoming more so in the face of climate change. When you compare the value of these services to the sovereign debt of the countries that are home to those forests it becomes clear that it's in the interest of rich countries to provide debt forgiveness in exchange for the conservation and restoration of the ecosystems that provide those services.'

The World Bank has also been working on embedding environmental outcomes into the broader government bond market, mirroring the rise of companies issuing 'green bonds' to help pay for corporate decarbonisation pledges. 'There's basically a penalty in the interest rate a country is charged if they don't meet, say, a national emissions reduction target, but their investors charge a lower interest rate initially. Investors are starting to acknowledge that it's less risky to lend to a country that is transitioning to a low-carbon, nature-positive economy and they are sharing some of the cost savings from that risk mitigation with the borrower. Issuing one of these bonds creates a real fiscal incentive for the government to meet the target,' Power explained.

In 2022, Chile became the first country to raise a $2 billion **sustainability-linked bond** tied to reducing emissions and increasing the country's share of renewable energy.[10] Power raised the prospect of doing the same for biodiversity outcomes, with the aim of 'protecting the global public goods from nature that we all take for granted'.

As we've seen with both rhino bonds and debt-for-nature swaps, philanthropic money can play a catalytic role in financial innovation. New initiatives are springing up to coordinate and direct donor funding better. This isn't limited to well-funded Western non-profits: Shloka Nath, Executive Director of the India Climate Collaborative (ICC), a non-profit, told me of her journey to setting up the ICC to direct catalytic donor funding in India. 'We asked ourselves: how do we build that next set of climate champions for India? Cumulative philanthropic spending in India on climate as well as its adjacent sectors stands at about $300 million. The [funding] gap is massive, but what we realised was that climate and nature were just less well understood,' she said. 'We had to bring solutions to donors and curate opportunities for them in the climate space based on the most urgent needs.' The ICC is building a portfolio of nature-based projects, using philanthropic cash to do the groundwork that can make projects attractive to private investors. In this way, donor money can play an important role in seeding proofs-of-concept, which will in turn help build investor comfort in financial innovations that can, at first, seem outlandish.

While international organisations and governments are reimagining the role of bonds and loans in financing a nature-positive future, others are taking a long, hard look at the structure of the common-stock company itself: that engine of economic growth that has, since the days of mercantilism, allowed managers to raise capital from investors to fuel growth and innovation.

When I first heard of the Intrinsic Exchange Group (IEG), I will admit I was puzzled by their proposition to create a new type of company they call a 'natural asset company (NAC)' in partnership with the New York Stock Exchange (NYSE).

The idea seemed to be that these NACs, an alternative to structuring these investments in nature as traditional companies or projects, would adopt a bespoke accounting system – Statements of Ecological Performance – as a parallel to the financial statements issued by regular corporations. NACs would both be a store of value and a way to capture the economic benefits of the many ecosystem services that lands, whether natural or working, can produce. As lands are preserved or restored, positive externalities (carbon, biodiversity, clean air and water, and so on) could be translated into financial capital, through avenues like sustainable sourcing, carbon and other ecosystem-service markets. The underlying assets could appreciate, much as a house does, to reflect restoration efforts.

Douglas Eger, Chairman and CEO of IEG, explained why he had gone down this alternative path, and how IEG had convinced that august institution of the old guard, the NYSE, to team up with them.

Eger urged me to think beyond the constraints of the finance and accounting classes I had sat through. 'A lot of what people are valuing with natural capital isn't captured by traditional accounting standards. Why do we accept this [model] as the only way we can create wealth – this model of "I have inputs of material and labour. I sell a product. Magically, I have profit."?'

The basic principle of IEG's new model looks like this: a company might list its agricultural land as an NAC, with shareholders buying into the new company to participate in its growth. Over time, regenerative agricultural practices might improve the underlying value of the land and generate eco-system services that would be detailed in the NAC's ecological statements. The NAC's share price would be designed to go up, and inventors could trade stocks in NACs freely, as they do with traditional companies. The core of this would be a company that values its natural capital fully and gets rewarded financially for improving its stocks and flows.

Eger explained the practical benefits for a cooperative of farmers who might want to go down the NAC route. 'To fund regenerative agriculture, for instance, there can be a small premium. But you have to find a way to include the production of ecosystem services along with commodity crops. The NAC model [enables] the financing of on-farm changes, the supply chain, and delivers to the end user an improved product.'

Unlike some other natural finance innovators we've met, Eger was insistent that a new paradigm for the stock-market itself was necessary to bring natural markets to life. To him, the creation of Natural Asset Companies was a necessary evolution of the natural capital framework we've explored in this book, by adapting balance sheets to include natural capital, rather than describing natural risks and impacts using only the existing language of traditional finance.

If IEG and NYSE are able to pull off this seemingly outlandish idea, it seems likely that the financial ecosystem would be better off. Perhaps, one day soon, the initial public offering bell at the New York Stock Exchange will ring regularly for NACs committed to restoring the planet, and provide a welcome break from the apparently endless march of consumer-products companies selling their greenwashed visions of growth and prosperity to would-be investors.

With the fate of the planet at stake, we have to be willing to go out on a limb for some of these financial innovations. When the Dutch East India Company (*Vereenigde Oost-Indische Compagnie* or VOC) conducted the world's first IPO in 1602, it must surely have been met with puzzlement and scepticism.[11] Those sceptics may well have felt vindicated as the stock price soared and collapsed in the tulip bubble that followed. But the VOC ultimately carried on until the turn of the nineteenth century, by which time the joint stock corporation had become the unshakeable global default.

There are other features of the financial system that may well be worth adapting to nature-positive business models. One that stands out is the system of ratings agencies, the S&P Global and Moody's of the world, that allow investors to assess corporate credit risk independently and virtually instantly. London-based start-ups BeZero and Sylvera, along with US-based Renoster, are examples of a new breed of ratings agencies, combining tech-enabled ecosystem monitoring with diligent analytical work to create global ratings agencies tailored to the voluntary carbon market.

BeZero, for instance, has rated hundreds of projects in much the same way as a traditional financial player might do for corporate balance sheets; a AAA-rated project might have, in their words, a 'high likelihood of achieving 1 tonne of CO_2e avoidance or removal', as opposed to an A-rated project with a 'low' likelihood. BeZero have appraised all sorts of projects, from a peatland conservation project in Indonesia that was rated AAA to a clean cookstove project in Guatemala that received a lowly A.

'When we first looked at the voluntary carbon market, there was absolutely zero correlation between our assessment of the quality of the carbon project and the price per tonne that was being charged… so that reflects a complete lack of transparency within the marketplace,' Nick Atkinson, Chief Science Officer at BeZero, told me. My own experience of the carbon markets confirmed this assessment: investing in the first wave of carbon projects was akin to buying a stock or bond with no idea about the underlying financial performance or credit rating of a company – not unheard of in the heady days of the pandemic stock-trading boom, but certainly not ideal for the functioning of a healthy market.

'The idea is that we can provide a dispassionate rating for the carbon impact of the project, and that then gives transparency to the investor or the buyer of that carbon tonne. They know that if they see a carbon credit that's rated at a lower level, they might have to buy two credits for every time that they want to offset.' Ratings agencies often get things wrong, as the main financial agencies did during the 2008 crisis; still, they constitute an important tool for investors and buyers who lack the ability to deeply assess each individual project.

Philip Platts, BeZero's Head of Earth Observation and an ecologist by training, was most concerned about the impact of an opaque carbon market on conservation outcomes. 'If good projects aren't getting well rewarded and aren't being well run, then that's a hindrance to conservation. On the flipside, if they can be well run and the price of a carbon credit can be more accurately linked to a good that it's doing in terms of carbon, and in terms of livelihoods as well, it can become a massive vehicle for making inroads for conservation.' For now, BeZero is focused on carbon markets, but rating co-benefits for UN Sustainable Development Goals or biodiversity are next on their list.

* * *

Reflecting on the world of traditional finance, with all its depth and liquidity, I was left wondering what these emerging analogues for nature-based finance had to do to be taken seriously.

Zach Knight told me Blue Forest had grappled with the same question, and that it partly came down to better evidence and communication. 'We need to draw from financing concepts that already work, that have a place in somebody's mind. That's not a finance or a science challenge. It's a communications challenge. Ultimately, you are educating investors and you're learning yourself how to better communicate what it is that these programs look like as we translate policy into finance.'

Nature, of course, can't be financed in exactly the same way as grey infrastructure. 'There are positives and negatives to green infrastructure,' Knight said. 'What's different is that the cash flows aren't as obvious. There is not a toll that someone's going to pay on the forest. So we need to get creative in how we engage different stakeholders and understand what success means for them.'

Some nature-positive financing pioneers, like the IEG team, are looking to break open the boxes that contain traditional finance. While efforts such as theirs pick up, it feels worthwhile, and at the very least pragmatic, to help nature speak the language of the current financial system. 'How do you make everything look more like a typical infrastructure project financing, where you've got a power purchase agreement and some sort of offtake agreement? How do we make these projects look and feel like other infrastructure investments? I think that's been in the DNA of Blue Forest since day one,' Knight explained.

As valuable as these financial innovations may be, they often sit between public and private control, which explains why many that we've explored here rely for the moment on making the case to a coalition of public and private investors, and bridging the yawning gap that can often exist between them.

'Finance people, for the most part, underestimate the power of government; and government people don't understand or underestimate the power of finance,' Knight pointed out. He himself had undergone a Damascene conversion to the power of the public purse. 'The thing that never occurred to me when I worked on trading floors or in finance was the power of policy and the scale at which government operates. That's why I think it's so powerful to have the government involved.'

Finance is ultimately a means to an end. If that end is the maximisation of short-term private profit with no regard for the ecological or social costs, and those are the values we choose to express through the financial system, that is exactly what the system will deliver. For myself, learning about the innovations of nature-positive finance, I feel cautiously hopeful that a different paradigm might be within reach: one that takes the financial ingenuity that animates the economic system, applies it to protect our planet's life support systems instead, and leaves us and our only home better off in the process.

The Indigenous
Case for Nature

Stepping off the ferry from downtown Auckland felt like stepping back in time to a primordial New Zealand. Ferns blanketed the forest floor. Birds of every hue ruled the roost, some flitting through the canopy, others appearing more than content with their flightlessness. Over the course of a summer, I had experienced what must have been the world's most pictur-esque commute, making daily research trips to Tiritiri Matangi island to study its rare wildlife and learn from the community that had helped bring this sanctuary to life. Field surveys with wide-eyed visitors were followed by lunch on a grassy hill with panoramic views of the Hauraki Gulf, surrounded by colourful *pūkeko* birds hoping to nab any leftovers.

The time I spent in New Zealand and among other indigenous communities elsewhere opened my eyes to a more ancient notion of nature rooted in indigenous wisdom and a sense of the planet's inherent pricelessness. After all, 80 per cent of the world's intact ecosystems are said to be found on indigenous land; even today, these indigenous-managed areas cover more of the Earth's surface than all of our national parks combined.[1,2]

Rather than seeing humans and nature as separate, these traditional belief systems have converged on the idea that the two are inextricably bound together. This stands in contrast to the colonial conversationist approach, which, as I described in the opening pages of this book, tends to see the Earth's flora and fauna as something to be fenced off and admired from afar. Virtually all have achieved thousands of years of mostly peaceful coexistence with biodiversity (even if extinctions the world over show that this narrative is far from one-dimensional). Even as we accept or reconcile with the constraints of a market system, indigenous cultures show us a way forward for living in kinship with the earth.

This isn't to say that the economic case for nature is always aligned with indigenous worldviews. It isn't, even if there are far more similarities than might at first meet the eye. Instead, indigenous worldviews remind us to see economics as no more than a practical and timely complement to the eternal, timeless value of nature. The two taken together offer a path forward from the high-minded Western fortress conservation ethos – the old model of booting original residents off their land and fencing off national parks while everything outside those boundaries is left to the forces of extractive capitalism – that has failed to forestall the planetary mess we now have on our hands.

Like many parts of the world, New Zealand was once a British settler-colony, subjected to the sadly standard abuses of suppression, settlement and extraction. But colonialism in Aotearoa, as New Zealand is known in Māori, had a markedly different opening act from neighbouring Australia.[3] The latter had been declared *terra nullius* by European settlers; its Aboriginal population were 'granted' few rights and treated effectively as subhuman.

In Aotearoa, two decades of contact and friction between the British and the native Māori people was followed by the Treaty of Waitangi, signed in 1840 with terms that sound, on paper, vaguely progressive even today. The letter of the treaty between the Crown and Māori chiefs from the North Island gave the latter full rights and protections as British subjects, alongside 'Lands and Estates, Forests, Fisheries and other properties which they may collectively or individually possess'.

Unsurprisingly, the Crown violated the spirit of the treaty soon thereafter and the Māori *iwi*, or tribes, found themselves marginalised on the land they had inhabited for hundreds of years. But, over time, the document proved remarkably resilient, setting out a legal basis for somewhat more equal relations. Eventually, in 1975, a Waitangi Tribunal was set up and awarded settlements of nearly NZD$2.2 billion for wrongs committed by the colonisers: a pittance compared to the damage wrought, but a far cry from the tone of the reparations debate in places like the US.[4] The modern-day Aotearoa I had the privilege of conducting my research in was visibly progressive (if far from perfect) in its embrace of the indigenous cultures that had predated colonialism.

Tiritiri is a distinctive case of community-led regeneration that had created a sanctuary for rare and endangered species of all sorts, as well as an accessible educational experience for city dwellers looking to connect with the country's natural wealth. I had come both to study Titiriti's bird populations and learn about the rich culture of Aotearoa's Māori people, closely bound as it was to the natural wonders of their islands.

Like many island nations, Aotearoa's native species had been decimated by ravenous invasives that were no longer subject to the natural population control exerted by predators in their native ecosystems. First came the (likely inadvertent) introduction of the Polynesian rat with the Māori in the thirteenth century; then came a more destructive wave of cats, weasels and the like alongside European settlers. The story of Tibbles, a lighthouse-keeper's cat that played an outsize, if not definitive, role in the extinction of the Stephens Island wren, only served to illustrate how profound an effect even small numbers of invasive species had had on a bird population unaccustomed to mammal predators.[5] The invaders had been successfully ejected from only a few islands such as Tiritiri, turning them into protective havens for the country's native wildlife.

As I trained to lead guided tours of the island, my manager Mary-Ann suggested I skip straight to the Māori names for the island's residents. 'You could use the English names, I suppose... but to me they just sound so inadequate when we're describing these beautiful birds.'

So I learnt that the little yellow-and-black honey-eating stitchbird was the *hihi*; the chubby rainbow-coloured swamphens that numbered just over 400 across the country were the *takahē*,

An endangered *takahē* on Tiritiri Matangi island.

while their far more common cousins were the *pūkeko*; the obnoxiously loud saddleback with its distinctive red wattles was the *tīeke*. Plants wore their indigenous names better too: *pohutukawa*, rather than the curiously anglocentric 'New Zealand Christmas tree'; *ponga* for the silver fern that was emblazoned across the country's sports insignia.

Diving deeper into Māori conceptions of nature provided welcome relief from the clinical work of field surveys along the winding paths and windswept clearings that dotted the island.

From the brilliant Māori and Pākehā (non-Māori) conservationists I worked with, I learnt that Māori take their responsibilities as stewards of the environment seriously, regarding nature with a deep respect and protecting it not only because it sustains livelihoods, but because of traditional, spiritual or cultural associations which often outweigh material concerns. Take the principle of *kaitiakitanga*, which describes 'guarding and protecting the environment in order to respect ancestors and secure the future'. Part of this duty is pragmatic, but part comes from a collective desire to preserve the *mana*, or spiritual power, of their land. In the past, *kaitiakitanga* was practised by *kaitiaki* (guardians) enforcing *rāhui* (temporary bans or restrictions, for example on harvesting resources in an area) and protecting *wāhi tapu* (sacred places). Today, *kaitiaki* work to address environmental issues with the government, fight to include the principles of *kaitiakitanga* in legislation, and advocate for the intangible and sacred values of nature to be incorporated into law.

Taking something from the land or sea is, to Māori, a privilege that comes with reciprocal responsibilities; in particular, the long-term responsibility as *kaitiaki* to guard and protect natural resources for future generations.[6] Rather than thinking of humans as existing separately from, or in opposition to, our environment, the Māori ethos is founded on the belief that human wellbeing is innately intertwined with that of nature. Such a notion will be familiar to first nations peoples all over the world.

While this shares some features with Western conceptions of the intrinsic value of nature, there is one important philosophical difference that is worth highlighting. Even the most well-meaning Eurocentric nature-lovers of the old school view conservation through the lens of preservation, according to which human use is 'environmentally damaging or problematic, and in respect of customary use issues, unethical' in the words of one review by a team of Māori and Pākehā researchers.[7] Fortress conservation has resulted in some significant conservation successes, but many prominent failures and grossly inadequate progress overall; there is no getting around the fact that eight billion people need to live sustainably off the land.

The Eurocentric conservation view stands in contrast to the 'conservation for future use' ethos that animates indigenous relationships to nature. 'Use is not a sacrilege but can be an honouring of wildlife, or potentially even an added incentive to good environmental stewardship. In this view, humans are seen as a fully interacting component of ecosystems and moderate impacts of humans as natural,' the researchers write.[8]

For the majority of the Earth that exists outside of strictly protected areas, the indigenous conception of coexisting with a functioning ecology both for its own sake, and for our collective use, appears to be the one more likely to work.

Titiriti itself had been deforested to farm and graze sheep until 1970, when it became the subject of an intensive replanting effort that added 240,000 native trees. Once invasive predators had been banished from the little island, birds that had largely been lost from the mainland were translocated to the safety of Tiritiri – the *tieke*, the *hihi* and the *takahē* included. It is the more remarkable that all this was done not by contractors, but by dozens of volunteers who organised themselves into a conservation society, the Supporters of Tiririti Matangi, that continues to oversee the day-to-day running of the now-lush island. Māori and Pacific Islanders from the Auckland area were regular visitors.[9] My most memorable day on Tiritiri came when I guided a group of inner-city schoolchildren who had never seen the sea, despite growing up just a few miles from the lapping waves of the Hauraki Gulf.

Further south, the Department of Conservation (DoC) had begun to co-manage Stephens Island, the scene of Tibbles's alleged crime and now a sanctuary for the rare endemic Tuatara lizards that are the last of an order of reptiles that once roamed the Earth alongside the dinosaurs. Here, the local Māori *iwi* and the DoC had established a co-management arrangement on indigenous land, an arrangement later touted as a pragmatic and equitable way forward for conservation in Aotearoa more broadly.

These advances on conservation came against the backdrop of a broader reimagining of the relationship between New Zealand's indigenous culture and its modern society. Later, on Waitangi Day 2022, I was struck by the words of Tā Joe Williams, the first Māori supreme court justice. He pointed to signs small and large, from the singing of the national anthem in Māori by default to advances on legal and social issues, that mutual respect was gradually taking hold. 'It tells you something about who we are becoming. Not who we have become – we have a long way to go – but who we are becoming. Now we can say there's momentum behind the basic idea that *Māoritanga* [the way of life] is important not just to me, as a Māori, but to everybody.'[10]

Aotearoa's relationship with its indigenous culture, like its track record on environmental issues more broadly, remains far from perfect. But I left that summer with a sense of hope that this country was taking real steps towards squaring these challenging circles as it embraces an ecological worldview, drawn from Māoritanga, that emphasises protection, rather than destruction.

First Nations Australians have lived a rather different story from their counterparts in Aotearoa. Their colonial history is arguably far darker; current inequities with non-Indigenous populations are starker. There is, too, a different cultural context. For instance, while the Māori largely share a language, Aboriginal and Torres Strait Australians spoke over 250 languages and dialects at the time of European settlement, reflecting the diversity of cultures and Nations within this vast land. And unlike the Māori, who arrived from other Polynesian islands around 800 years ago, Aboriginal Australians settled in Australia at least 50,000 years ago.

That added up to a far older human imprint on Australia's flora and fauna. For millennia, Aboriginal Australians lit fires – central to traditional knowledge and culture – in a thoughtful and ecologically sensible way, as a land-management practice. 'Good things came from fire. It made the land comfortable, comforting, bountiful and beautiful,' academic historian Bill Gammage writes in *The Biggest Estate on Earth*. Aboriginal fire management was capable of 'sustaining more diversity than any natural fire regime could conceivably maintain [...] wild, devastating fire rarely arose. People had to prevent it or die. They worked hard to make fire malleable, and to confine killer fires to legends and cautionary tales.'[11] All of this came about thanks to a spiritual connection to the land, and ecological knowledge of where and when to light fires that had been passed down orally through the generations.

In short, Australia's modern ecology – the infamous koalas and kangaroos, and the trees and plants that sustain them – co-evolved with humans for millennia. Until, of course, the arrival of European settlers, who had as much fear of fire as they did disdain of the traditional practices that had managed it successfully.

John Kanowski, Chief Science Officer at the Australian Wildlife Conservancy (AWC), shed light on what ails Australia's fire-adapted ecosystems. 'Europeans came in with very different notions of fire. I myself come from a family of foresters, who brought with them this forestry ethos from Germany, where it was very much about fire being a threat that you kept out,' he said. 'Indigenous people were treated absolutely atrociously, but they were also basically banned from burning in the way they had done for thousands of years. The end result was a massive increase in fuel loads, and a wildfire cycle that we're still to get out of.'

How do small, controlled fires create, rather than destroy, habitats for wildlife? Beyond preventing larger and more uncontrollable wildfires by clearing flammable undergrowth, the burns create 'patchiness' in the landscape that allows multiple species of animals to find their own ecological niches. 'We only realised this after a fantastic study led by traditional owners who knew the land intimately. Even our best satellites have a minimum pixel size, but it turned out a lot of this life-sustaining heterogeneity was invisible to the tools available at the time.'

Ever-larger bushfires have raged across the continent as the planet warms and Australia grows drier. The Black Summer, the fire season of 2019–2020, scorched an area larger than Sri Lanka and released more carbon dioxide than the nation of Greece does in an entire year.[12] Images of charred wombats and koalas filled TV screens: an estimated three billion animals were harmed, alongside the 445 humans who died in connection with the blaze.[13]

In Northern Australia, the AWC and other organisations are attempting to turn back the clock on Australia's folly with respect to fire by reviving indigenous fire management practices and pairing them with modern equipment. In the Kimberly, for instance, the conservancy has partnered with the Wilinggin and Dambimangari Aboriginal Corporations. In a vast tropical savannah region known for its rugged landscapes and limestone cliffs, the AWC enlisted Aboriginal partners to join helicopter-equipped fire crews, fanning out over an area half the size of England to drop incendiary capsules to create controlled burns.

Farmers and ranchers who have previously shunned fire are approaching the AWC, seeking prescribed burns to protect their property from destruction. And new business models are being layered onto these ancient indigenous practices to create a stream of funding for restoration activity; scientists working with Aboriginal groups have developed a well-validated methodology that allows them to issue carbon credits. After all, small burns can prevent the larger wildfires that release far larger quantities of carbon dioxide into the air.

There are other groups who are championing the value of indigenous fire management across the world, from Canada to Namibia to Brazil. I visited the Pantanal the year after a catastrophic series of wildfires had ripped through the wetland, exacerbated by climate change but enabled by ecologically unsound fire suppression on ranches. 'The authorities and recent settlers see fire as being the enemy. Fire is not the enemy. You have to know how to use fire in a wise way, just as the old guard [of European settlers] in the Pantanal did for 250 years, and the native population did for centuries before them,' Andre of Araras lodge had told me, decrying those who either suppressed fire and let straw build up on the grasslands, or burnt in the dry season, against traditional wisdom, when the flames could burn out of control.

It can be tempting to see indigenous practices in isolation – as how-to guides for managing ecosystems that anyone can take up and replicate. But the most successful programmes that lean on these techniques emphasise the importance of indigenous land tenure and self-determination; elements that are scarcer in Southern Australia, I learned. 'It is a different story in Southern Australia because the dispossession of indigenous people has happened for much longer. Fire management is a cultural artefact, not an innate skill [...] If people are separated from their practices, even just for a generation, they can disappear,' Kanowski pointed out.

All over the world, colonialism encouraged the displacement and cultural assimilation of indigenous peoples and precipitated – intentionally or not – the withering away of their languages, cultures and traditional practices. But this colonising mindset is not yet the preserve of history books. In India, despite progressive laws, constitutional protections and decades of activism, over a million Adivasi forest-dwellers face eviction from their traditional lands to advance a fortress-conservation model that sees them as obstacles rather than allies.[14] In Kenya, the forest service is reported to have carried out a series of violent evictions of the Sengwer community from their ancestral glades even as Covid-19 raged in the country; in neighbouring Tanzania, thousands of indigenous Maasai faced eviction in 2022 over plans for a new hunting lodge.[15, 16] These are but three examples of the innumerable territorial losses and indignities that indigenous peoples across the world must endure to this day.

Movements to secure indigenous sovereignty have gathered steam in recent years. In 2017, the Uluru Statement from the

Heart, the largest-ever consensus statement by Australian First Nations peoples, declared that 'sovereignty is a spiritual notion: the ancestral tie between the land, or "mother nature", and the Aboriginal and Torres Strait Islander peoples who were born therefrom, remain attached thereto, and must one day return thither to be united with our ancestors [...] It has never been ceded or extinguished and co-exists with the sovereignty of the Crown.[...] We seek constitutional reforms to empower our people and take *a rightful place* in our own country. When we have power over our destiny our children will flourish. They will walk in two worlds and their culture will be a gift to their country.'[17]

Unsurprisingly, study after study has shown that securing indigenous land tenure can help protect and restore natural ecosystems. The 370 million indigenous peoples around the world legally hold 18 per cent of the world's land, much of it in biodiversity hotspots that we collectively need to protect at all costs.[18] Researchers looking at indigenous-managed lands in Bolivia, Brazil and Colombia have found that they generate tremendously valuable ecosystem services, worth hundreds of billions of dollars, with the costs of securing them representing at most 1 per cent of the total benefits.[19] A landmark study of Brazilian conservation outcomes from 2005 to 2012 found that deforestation rates on indigenous territories were as much as seventeen times lower than in unprotected areas, contrary to age-old stereotypes that insinuate that the reverse is true.[20]

Reversing dispossession and granting formal rights over land previously lacking in legal title may be driving these nature-positive outcomes. One clever study used the staggered timing of indigenous title grants in Brazil to estimate their *causal* effects on deforestation, finding that collective property rights reduced deforestation by about 75 per cent. With over 2 million hectares of indigenous land still awaiting such titling, these findings will only add volume to the chorus of voices calling to secure as quickly as possible the rights of the world's first nations peoples to the land they have always stewarded.[21]

Nia Tero is one organisation that has emerged to enable the assertion of such tenure. Working across the Amazon, the Pacific Islands and the Boreal forests of Canada, Nia Tero 'forges transparent and just agreements with Indigenous peoples and local communities to ensure they can successfully defend and govern their territories, manage and protect their natural resources, and pursue their livelihoods.'[22]

Peter Seligmann, who founded the global conservation non-profit Conservation International in 1987, was instrumental in creating Nia Tero. 'We had conserved 300 or 400 million acres over decades of work at CI, and I remember thinking, "Gosh, that's a lot".' Seligmann explained. 'And then I looked at the globe, and what we had protected was about the width of that perforated line around the middle. I spent a lot of time thinking about scale and learnt that a third of the Earth is under the guardianship of indigenous peoples. Some of it is formal tenure, some informal. But I learnt that those places were extremely important for climate with 20 to 30 per cent of the above ground carbon, half of the tropical forests, 80 per cent of biodiversity, 40 per cent of intact ecosystems,' he said. 'And almost zero per cent of the financial support. And so I concluded that, to get to scale, we had to focus on supporting indigenous peoples, and give up our power to their authority and ownership and wisdom.'

Founded in 2017, Nia Tero now hosts an unconventional mix of capabilities in service of its mission, bringing indigenous leaders from fields as disparate as the arts and the legal profession under its umbrella. The organisation works to secure long-term stewardship both by advancing supportive policies and by telling stories that uplift indigenous voices and expand global understanding of indigenous wisdom. Ta Joe Williams, who so powerfully captured Aotearoa's national journey, now chairs Nia Tero.

Nia Tero's storytelling division, led by Tracy Rector, who is of Choctaw and African American heritage, has chalked up many successes, including a co-production, *What They've Been Taught*, that premiered at Sundance in 2022. 'It's just the beginning. I see storytelling as a way to elevate an understanding of indigenous perspectives on reciprocity, to a non-indigenous audience… so they can grow to understand and support indigenous calls for land tenure and other things. We're going to need allies, and we're going to have to capture the hearts and minds of non-indigenous people,' Seligmann said.

But indigenous rights and assets go beyond territory. In some cases, traditional knowledge – natural intellectual property, if you will – can also be part of the equation.

The case of rooibos, the distinctive amber-red tea from South Africa, illustrates how the ground might finally be shifting. Rooibos ('red bush' in Afrikaans) had been consumed by the Khoi and San peoples of the Western Cape for generations and was first commercialised around 150 years ago by colonial South African settlers. While we know it best in tea form, there are currently in excess of 140 patents pending for its biochemical and health properties, many of which have been inferred from the traditional knowledge that led the Khoi and San to use it in the first place.

Global efforts to secure the benefits of such knowledge for indigenous peoples – including the UN's 1992 Convention on Biological Diversity and the 2010 Nagoya Protocol – have unfortunately done little to create rules for benefit sharing. We frown upon copycat businesses that nab intellectual property from film studios or clothing brands; why should specialist indigenous knowledge be any different?

In 2019, the now-thriving rooibos industry pioneered a new approach to sharing the fruits of natural intellectual property, agreeing a broad benefit-sharing agreement with the Khoi and San peoples. An annual levy of 1.5 per cent on the price of rooibos leaving farms in the Western Cape is now paid out to communities, who have put in place governance and equitable distribution mechanisms for these benefits. Researchers credit the patience, incrementalism and dialogue of the parties involved for creating what has become a global first for indigenous peoples seeking just a sliver of the benefits their traditional knowledge can bring to businesses and governments.[23]

Some places have taken legal innovation even further, extending protection beyond the human stewards of nature to the rights of nature itself.

Aotearoa once again shows the way. In 2017, the Whanganui River, the country's third longest, was recognised as a legal person. As out-there as that may sound to those who have only ever heard of legal personhood in the Western sense, the change was demanded in response to English property rights that had carved the river and its banks up into various parts. To the Māori *iwi* who inhabited the area, the river was an indivisible whole with its own life force, or *mauri*. The Waitangi Tribunal eventually stepped in, declaring that the river had rights of its own and appointing two guardians to speak on its behalf.

Why did the Māori want this recognition for *Te Awa Tupua*, the worldview that considered the river to be a living whole? Expressly not to prevent economic activity or sanction those who use it, but to consider such use from a central belief that fits with their traditional notion of nature, one that both gives and is deserving of human giving.[24]

Ecuador's 2008 constitution, voted into law by a majority of its citizens, did something similar when it gave *Pachamama*, or Mother Earth, legally enforceable rights including the right to 'maintain and regenerate its cycles, structure, functions and evolutionary processes'. In 2021, the country's constitutional court put this into practice, ordering the government to revoke mining permits in the severely threatened Los Cedros cloud forest to protect the ecosystem's rights.[25]

Progress hasn't been as linear elsewhere. In India, the high court in the Himalayan state of Uttarakhand cited the Whanganui case to grant the Ganga and Yamuna rivers, long considered sacred by Hindus, legal personhood in 2017.[26] The move followed years of judicial activism aimed at stemming the torrent of pollutants streaming into the two rivers; however, India's Supreme Court suspended the order later that year, calling it legally unsustainable.[27]

Albeit progressing in fits and starts, the rights-of-nature movement seeks to rethink humanity's relationship to nature more fundamentally than many of us might imagine possible. While legal frameworks can in general play an important role in encouraging us to value, rather than exploit, nature, these moves have to date been largely symbolic. But symbolism can matter, even if all it does is shift the Overton window to make other environmental protections appear more 'moderate' by comparison. Beyond the outcomes, the very fact that indigenous worldviews are finally being lent credence in the eyes of the law, at least in some places and on some measures, is surely worth celebrating.

Reflecting on what I have learnt from indigenous peoples' framing of the nature question, a few important themes stand out.

For one, the very notion of wilderness appears to melt away as I read paper after paper documenting the deep human imprint that tens of thousands of years of walking the Earth have left on it. There are certainly places where that imprint is less destructive – often the places where indigenous peoples have found longstanding ways of thriving alongside plants and animals. I also find myself recoiling from language that "others" First Nations peoples; casting them as blameless and noble feels like a patronising oversimplification. Even the Māori, when they first settled in Aotearoa, had hunted giant flightless Moa birds to extinction before they arrived at an ethos of coexistence that fitted their new surroundings.

Today, indigenous guardians of the natural world live off the land at the same time as they exist within wider market economies; trade-offs exist for them just as they do for small-holder farmers and business owners alike.

Those trade-offs can resolve themselves in ways that might seem unacceptable to the Western conservation ethos, from small-scale polar bear hunting by the Inuit to the continued use of fire as landscape management in the Australian bush. In other cases, centuries of marginalisation and a persistent lack of economic opportunity have led indigenous peoples to make hard decisions about the land they inhabit. The Native Americans who have opened up their lands to mining and drilling have surely done so with heavy hearts. That said, indigenous groups in different regions around the world may perceive economic opportunities in relation to their lands in differing ways. As Peter Seligmann points out, 'Indigenous peoples are not homogenous. For instance, there's a loud voice, especially in the US, that is anticapitalist and distrustful of motives. And you can understand why. Trust is essential, and Indigenous peoples have little reason to trust the outside or commercial world. History is littered with examples of broken promises. The position that most indigenous peoples are taking is that this diversity of opinions allows [their] communities to make their own choices.'

Beyond economics, researching and writing this chapter has renewed my profound respect for the indigenous cultures, practices and worldviews that have too often been lost in the debate on saving our planet. The spiritual connection to nature that binds many of these disparate Nations together feels important, timely and inspiring even to those of us who do not consider ourselves indigenous.

In an intimate portrait of the Koyukon Athabascan First Nations peoples of Alaska, cultural anthropologist Richard Nelson offers an outsider's translation of that culture's view of nature in terms that resonated deeply with me. The Koyukon worldview is one of *relationship* to nature rather than monolithic devotion or utilitarian resource-management; it treats plants and animals in the same way as family members. Family relationships can be life-giving, but they can also be contentious, and the Koyukon seek to navigate this complexity based on a deep respect, shunning the transactional approach that, as most of us know all too well, can damage relationships.[28]

Seeing ourselves as custodians of our living planet through deep time can lead us to make decisions differently: sustainability takes on a deeper meaning when it operates on millennial, rather than quarterly, timescales. I will admit that learning about this perspective even led me to question the framing of this book around business cases for nature rather than the timeless value of nature. I was led to interrogate more forcefully my embrace of pragmatism to make progress now, rather than doing the hard yards of reimagining our entire relationship with nature.

But a series of conversations – and sometimes more heated debates – revealed areas of common ground between the two approaches, in addition to those obvious areas of tension. The ecosystem services that economics currently values are the ones that tend to involve the extraction of oil, timber, fish and the like. Indigenous cultures instead value the broader suite of life-giving services that have, until now, been largely ignored by capitalism. In some respects, these indigenous notions might have more in common with the natural capital thinking that animates this book – those of deeply valuing and sustainably harnessing the entire spectrum of services that nature provides, while investing in their future provision – than the arm's-length relationship to nature that both colonial-style conservation and unchecked extraction share.

It also seems to me that the various business cases we have explored, from community-based carbon credit projects to thoughtful ecotourism, could finally offer a way out of the Hobson's choices that indigenous groups often face when attempting to pair economic and social development with cultural integrity. If First Nations are truly able to make free and informed choices along those lines, as the UN Declaration on the Rights of Indigenous Peoples calls for, why shouldn't they be able finally to receive some financial support in return for the public goods the lands they steward provide to the whole planet?

Natural capital could finally recognise, in admittedly market-based terms, a small slice of the universe of practical, cultural and spiritual value that nature brings. It might offer indigenous peoples a way to stem the tide of no-holds-barred financial capitalism by creating business models that rely on regeneration rather than exploitation. And if they choose to reject business cases for nature in favour of long-term conservation for its own sake, non-indigenous actors must accept that this is entirely within their rights too, in the spirit of mutual respect and self-determination that must lie at the heart of such engagements. It would only be right after so many wrongs.

Synthesis

After you have exhausted what there is in business, politics, conviviality, and so on — have found that none of these finally satisfy, or permanently wear — what remains? Nature remains.

— Walt Whitman

Many years ago, I spent a day in my conservationist grandmother's library, reading about reefs and reptiles, my wonderment at the richness of the natural world growing by the hour. When my grandmother returned that evening, I tried, gushing with excitement, to recount to her what I had learnt. Clearly, I wasn't making much sense. 'I'm not sure I understand, *kanna*. Explain that to me again, as you would to a child, using just three words,' she suggested, unbothered by the fact that I was myself a child at the time.

In wrapping up this book, dedicated in part to my grand-mother's memory, I remembered that day and thought I might try the same technique. I grasped around, searching for the right simple words that could summarise what I wanted to communicate. In the end, I alighted on four words – *from*, *in*, *with*, and *as* (nature) – that I found in the seemingly unpromising ground of an IPBES report.

The cornerstone of the economic case for nature is a meaningful recognition of our essential dependence on nature: the fact that we are all living *from* nature. For too long, nature has been seen as natural only if it is also pristine and at one remove from the dirty business of everyday human dealings, the preserve of documentaries and postcards. This thinking is little more than a fantasy, and a dangerous one at that, feeding the notion that we have somehow decoupled ourselves and our modern economy from dependence on the natural world.

Human societies and economies can only survive and thrive, in the long term, thanks to the natural world; thanks to the physical goods nature provides us, from food to fuel and timber; and thanks to regulating and supporting ecosystem services, from pollination to carbon storage and flood protec-tion. For too long, these many facets have been ignored and cast aside, in favour of a short-term, extractive view.

The pragmatic case for nature also extends to how we live *in* nature, be that in the countryside or in an urban jungle. Our lives are made healthier and happier by bringing nature into our lives, be it through trips to faraway isles or walks through city parks. That nature is good for our wellbeing is no surprise; that it can bring practical and economic benefits to communities and governments only makes the case for nature even more compelling.

But we've known that we live *from* and *in* nature for decades – it hasn't prevented the twin tragedies of the commons and the horizon from diverting us from a sensible path. What's different today, as this book sets out, are the pioneers who are making the economic case for nature in new and transformative ways. I thought back to the tireless work of Gretchen in Palo Alto, Wilson and Viraj in Selenkay, Jone and Marina in Taveuni, Zach in Tahoe, and the many others I encountered. Pioneers can also be found in cities as far apart as Singapore and Medellín; in companies as large and established as Microsoft and as new as IEG. Not all these efforts might achieve global scale, but these are the many faces of a revolution that is being enabled by thoughtful policies and exciting new leaps in technology and finance.

From carbon markets and ecotourism to nature-positive agriculture and urban greening, each of them is proving that a better way of living from and in nature is possible, not at some distant point in the future, but now. Their stories deserve to be told far and wide, and we'll return to the ways in which you can help.

* * *

As underappreciated as those first two words – which amount to an extrinsic, or economic, framing – are, the latter two matter profoundly as well.

Living *with* and *as* nature is what will anchor us, and act as a moral and spiritual compass, even as we forge ahead in making the pragmatic, economic case that has been too long overlooked.

Living ***with*** nature – in harmony with nature, as stewards of nature, perhaps even securing the rights of nature – is the case that all the world's wisest traditions have made for millennia. It is an idea that encourages us to see nature as the basis of our culture and ourselves as uniquely sentient beings, the products of billions of years of evolution, with a special responsibility to protect everything else with which we share our planet. We must embrace and cultivate our sense of ecological and cosmic particularity and responsibility, underpinned by whatever system of faith or morality we choose.

Finally comes perhaps the boldest proposition of all – that we can live ***as*** nature, as many indigenous traditions seek to do. In this framing, we might begin to see ourselves reflected in nature, embracing the deepest of spiritual connections with the diversity of life on Earth. In protecting nature, we protect ourselves.

This may be too big a leap for some. But I suspect each of you has felt, at one time or other, that sense of stewardship for the natural world, and understands that we can, in some deep sense, exist *as* nature.

We cannot afford to succumb to a false binary between the intrinsic and the economic frames, as Christiana Figueres emphasised. 'They're not two sides of a polarised world. To me, they're actually stacked on top of each other. So, when I think about the moral imperative [to protect nature], I put it right there right at the base. On top of that, you have the scientific imperative. You have the economic imperative [...] You just stack up all these imperatives, and the answer becomes clear.'

Those who contend that economic motivations weaken intrinsic ones forget that market forces already operate in these ecosystems: every poacher, illegal logger, intensive farmer, palm oil producer or fishing trawler is responding to a set of economic incentives that tilt towards overexploitation. The point that this book set out to make is simply that a different set of economic incentives is being fashioned as we speak; one that encourages, rather than militates against, our better angels. We will ultimately need to stack each of these ideas, of living *from*, *in*, *with* and *as* nature. Context may dictate which of the frames resonates more strongly, but they do, taken together, add up to a powerful case for nature.

In concluding, I decided not to offer prescriptions for the world at large to halt the climate and nature crisis. In any event, they tend to converge on a few well-worn, if still valid, exhortations:

for government policy to make markets work and to spend both generously and intelligently; for businesses to be ecologically sensitive, rather than rapacious, to create long-term shareholder and stakeholder value; for industrialised economies to cough up long-promised dollars to help the developing world.

Instead, I want to speak directly to you as we come to the end of this journey: to offer some principles that might be worth bearing in mind, and some actions to consider in your own personal and professional lives.

My own set of guiding principles will, by now, be familiar.

First, we can be constructive sceptics when assessing any case for nature, to guard against feel-good environmental stories that have little substance. I hope these chapters have given you some of the tools you need to be a discerning consumer of information; you now have a sense of the standards we can apply to ensure that carbon credits are robust, ecotourism properly supports conservation, and regenerative products are nature-positive. You now also know the degree of transparency that technology and financial tools can and should enable.

But when you and I demand radical transparency, we should do so with empathy. Not every misstep is malicious, and the people attempting to build nature-positive business models in their communities are usually good, honest individuals who are learning and growing along the way. Demand better of them, by all means, but try to avoid the vitriol and blanket denouncements that often do more harm than good.

Second, let's make sure to ask where the dollars ultimately flow. The case for nature is also the case for a regenerative, rather than extractive, economy. Following the money can help reveal whether these economic models are creating impact for the people and places that matter. Unscrupulous middlemen will always exist, particularly as new markets get set up; demanding that most of the money from your visit or purchase goes to the communities in question isn't too much to ask.

Third, we can remember the people behind it all. Enhancing human capital can be a powerful complement to securing natural capital, and there are many important intersections between the case for nature and the case for a more just, equal, anti-racist world. Improving the wellbeing of our societies is what will ultimately create durable support for environmental progress, and it feels fanciful to try and solve our broken relationship with nature without simultaneously healing the social contract between us humans. The best cases for nature happen to be the ones where locals give more than free, prior, informed consent, when they actively come together, as they did in creating the High Line or restoring Selenkay. Each of us can play a part in creating the conditions for change through our work, votes, community engagement and personal action.

By now, we have seen that policymakers, businesses and the finance sector can really move the needle on this existential challenge. If you occupy any of those roles, you have your work cut out in your professional life: you need to put nature firmly on your organisation's agenda and help retool as many processes and products as you can to support a net-zero, nature-positive economic model, using any of the business cases we've explored in this book.

Countless mission-driven individuals with a range of skills, from engineers to marketing professionals, are dedicating their careers to working directly on the climate and nature crisis. These roles span the largest companies and government departments to the smallest start-ups, funds and NGOs. If your personal circumstances justify it, you might consider joining their ranks; you could even start your own venture or initiative. As a first step, grassroots action may feel within reach. Like the citizens who campaigned for the High Line or are replanting Freetown, joining a community effort to restore nature can be personally energising and locally impactful.

As a citizen and consumer, you are the foundational building block of democratic capitalism. That gives you incredible *power*, even if *responsibility* ultimately lies with larger systems. That power – currently being used to ravage natural systems, with or without our knowledge – can be harnessed for precisely the opposite goal.

If you have made it to the end of this book, you've already taken one step towards understanding the multitude of cases for nature. While we have barely scratched the surface, I hope you will want to dive deeper into the rich world of nature-positive economic models.

As you learn, be sure to share your enthusiasm with those around you who likely also feel concern about seemingly unrelated issues, from animal welfare to plastic pollution and species extinctions. Talk of natural capital as an integrated whole, and spread the word that, much like the transition to a net-zero climate future, the case for nature also brings with it a chance for a brighter economic future. Climate change didn't jump onto the agenda of global leaders and chief executives out of nowhere. It took a million conversations, borne of thoughtful individuals learning and demanding better of their societies. I urge you to have those conversations once more, this time on behalf of nature.

If you have a talent for media of any sort, consider sparking those conversations by harnessing all the possibilities of our internet-connected world. When my friend Sophie Purdom decided to launch the Climate Tech VC newsletter in the depths of the pandemic, she happily admitted to doing so 'selfishly, from a desire to synthesise and make sense of the climate-tech world'. But the volunteer-run newsletter has quickly become a credible and trusted source for many in the climate start-up and investment community. 'All we did was figure out how to connect climate, and technology, with either your job today or your hopes for the future, and communicate that in an elevated, educated but still inspiring, accessible, and frankly punny way!'

If you live in a society lucky enough to host free and fair elections: use your vote. Politics can feel like a hopeless endeavour at times, but many of the cases I encountered in this book had been enabled by thoughtful government support. You can help elect allies at every level: city, state or national. They might fall short, but they might also make dramatic changes by harnessing the power of the state, as many committed public servants have done across the world. You might even choose to run someday.

You can even go one step further with activism and volunteering to play a part in building enthusiasm for nature within your communities. While doing so, keep in mind that the case for nature cannot come at the expense of climate action, where activism has indeed achieved remarkable results. The two movements are natural allies; the trade-offs, where they exist, can be resolved through the patient work of consultation, if only we keep our eyes on the better vision of the future that they ultimately share.

Just as the intrinsic and economic cases for nature complement each other, so too do small personal steps and demands for systemic change.

Those who can afford it can also vote with their wallets and diets. The money you spend has cascading effects that can extend halfway across the world, including to those pristine ecosystems we all dream of visiting. If you're reading this book, ivory, shark fins and old-growth teak are likely not on your shopping list, but our collective purchasing decisions have inadvertently created a powerful business case for investing in more cattle ranches, palm oil plantations, fishing trawlers and wildcat mines in the Amazon. None of this is sustainable, and businesses are beginning to realise as much – you can speed up their awakening by demanding better of them. By taking a hard look at your purchasing decisions, large or small, you signal that these impacts matter to you, and send a message about the nature-positive future you want.

Wherever you live, you can help bring nature back in ways small or large. When I spoke to Issy Tree and Charlie Burrell at Knepp, they emphasised to me that even a city dweller with a window box could help rewild a landscape, no Castle Estate required. In their new publication, *The Book of Wilding*, they offer a practical guide to rewilding at even the smallest of scales.

Perhaps the most important, and most personal, step is to cultivate the sense of wonder in nature that lives deep within all of us.

After spending years in the forests of Tanzania, shedding light on the social lives of our closest chimpanzee relatives, Jane Goodall wrote that, 'For those who have experienced the joy of being alone with nature there is really little need for me to say much more; for those who have not, no words of mine can even describe the powerful, almost mystical knowledge of beauty and eternity that come, suddenly, and all unexpected.

The beauty was always there, but moments of true awareness were rare.'[1]

Those moments of awareness may be rare, but they have been some of the most deeply motivating in my own journey of researching and writing this book. They came unannounced, just as Goodall said they would, sometimes on visits to far-flung locations that reflected my own enormous privilege, but sometimes also in the most pedestrian of settings. Looking out into the Indian ocean from monsoonal Mumbai, trekking on horseback through the verdant Pantanal, walking through some of the last fragments of primaeval forest in Devon: on each of those occasions, and so many others, I felt lucky to be alive and more committed than ever to speaking for nature.

I urge you to find more of those Jane Goodall moments in your lives. Whether in green spaces close to home, or further afield as a thoughtful ecotourist, allow yourself to feel, rather than merely think. I've noticed that the youngest members of our society understand this intuitively and express it in their love for animals or outdoor play. Regardless of how old we are, keeping alive the sense that we live *with* and *as* nature, that sense of the sublime, will underpin everything we do.

Where do we go from here? Each year seems to bring with it another urgent economic, public health or geopolitical crisis on top of rising tides and burning forests. But as I think back to places like Kanha and Komodo, I can't help but feel optimistic. To be sure, much has been lost. But so much remains to be saved and restored. By appealing to the economic and the intrinsic, the head and the heart, I feel more confident than ever in our ability to find a way, however tentative at first, to forge the nature-positive economies and societies of the future. At its heart, this story I've told, about Pacific sharks, urban parks and everything in between, is a story about the human ingenuity that is helping us overcome our all-too-human failings, and the ways in which we can, on this pale blue dot we call home, make the case for nature.

Acknowledgements

This book would simply not have been possible without the support of the many people who offered me their encouragement, time, networks, sound advice and support.

It all began with a last-minute proposal submitted to the *Financial Times*–McKinsey Bracken Bower Prize; I owe many thanks to Lorella Belli, who judged that prize and agreed to be my agent and help build on my proposal. I was lucky to be able to work with two brilliant editors, Rowan Cope of Duckworth and Manasi Subramaniam of Penguin Random House India, to bring this book to life.

Thanks to my research assistant, Angharad Morgan, for her patient and meticulous work; any errors remain my responsibility.

Writing this book was made all the more enjoyable by the friends who volunteered to provide feedback or keep me company on my travels: Aakash Ahamed, Aaran Patel, Amy Hammond, Alex Prather, Ben Kramer, Cath Berner, Chris Stromeyer, Dany Rifkin, Emily Fry, Eric Nevalsky, Frances Simpson-Allen, John Foye, Kobi Weinberg, Morrison Mast, Richard Ng, Siobhan Stewart, Sophie Purdom, Tommaso Cariati, Tyler Brandon, Vidit Doshi and so many others.

I drew on the wisdom of those far more experienced than me. Anne Simpson and Laura Hattendorf gave up countless hours of their time to offer sage advice on the manuscript. Alicia Sieger, Art Ward, Colin le Duc, Gretchen Daily, Gyanendra Badgaiyan, Hans Mehn, Henry Mance, Justin Adams, Mark Mills, Owen Lewis, Sayeqa Islam and Shannon Bouton helped shape my thinking on a range of topics and kindly opened up their contact books for me.

My parents laid the foundations for all of it. My father, Shrikanth, was my first teacher and mentor. I will never forget our long drives through the Indian countryside in my childhood, the hours flying by as he fed my curiosity about how the planet really works; he remains a sounding board and guiding light to this day. My mother, Vasanthy, taught me what unconditional love meant. She sacrificed so much as she raised us, dedicating her formidable energies to me and my sister until we had flown the nest. She is now a wildlife photographer and an inspiration both to me and to a new generation of conservationists in India and beyond. I could not be more grateful to them both.

My sister, Sushmitha, is an inspiration in her own right. In following her passion for yoga and philosophy, she made it possible for me to do the same with nature and played the dual roles of cheerleader and guinea-pig reader to great effect as I wrote this book. I know that she will always have my back, and I, hers.

I owe so much to Shyamli, whose unshakeable values, rare creative talents and powerful intellect have shaped me profoundly. She has helped me see what truly matters through her own quest to feel, think and make sense of the world. A life of learning, laughter, adventure and service feels within reach; this book, and so much else, would never have seen the light of day without her.

Further Reading

There are countless excellent books on nature and climate that have helped educate and inspire me. See below for a short, non-exhaustive reading list in case you're eager for more.

Narratives on Nature and Climate

- *The Invention of Nature* by Andrea Wulf (John Murray, 2015) – the fascinating biography of Alexander von Humboldt, a polymath who perhaps invented our modern conception of nature
- *Under a White Sky* by Elizabeth Kolbert (Vintage, 2021) – a hard look at the imprint we're leaving on the planet
- *How to Love Animals* by Henry Mance (Vintage, 2021) – a witty and non-judgemental inquiry into why we treat animals so badly

- *Race for Tomorrow* by Simon Mundy (William Collins, 2021) – a travelogue that lays bare the real-world impacts of climate change and ecological collapse from Siberia to the Solomon Islands
- *What's Left of the Jungle* by Nitin Sekar (Bloomsbury India, 2022) – a close-up look at the challenges of conservation and human–wildlife conflict in India
- *The Uninhabitable Earth* by David Wallace-Wells (Penguin, 2019) – a brief but devastatingly lucid summary of the science of the climate emergency
- *Wilding* by Isabella Tree (Picador, 2018) and *Land Healer* by Jake Fiennes – (BBC Books, 2022) both tell stories of life returning to British farms
- *Regenesis* by George Monbiot (Penguin, 2022) – a manifesto for how we might transform farming and make space for nature
- *Braiding Sweetgrass* by Robin Wall Kimmerer (Milkweed Editions, 2013 and Penguin, 2020) – a lyrical memoir that sheds light on indigenous wisdom and the teachings of plants

Practical Guides on Nature and Climate
- *Valuing Nature* by William Ginn (Island Press, 2020) and *The Little Book of Investing in Nature* (Global Canopy, 2020) – two handbooks for investing in nature that feature a wealth of case studies

- ***Green Growth That Works*** (Island Press, 2019) – a guide to natural capital mechanisms across policy and finance
- ***How to Avoid a Climate Disaster*** by Bill Gates (Penguin, 2021) – a clear and accessible guide to the basics of de-carbonising the planet
- ***Regeneration: Ending the Climate Crisis in One Generation*** by Paul Hawken (Penguin, 2021) – a menu of actions to reverse climate change and biodiversity loss

Notes

Why Nature? Why Now?

1   Hausfather, Z. (2021). *State of the climate: 2020 ties as warmest year on record*. Carbon Brief. (Online) Available at: https://tinyurl.com/2p8m-jwt4 [Accessed: 15th July 2022]
2   Wallace-Wells, D. (2019). *The uninhabitable Earth: A story of the future*. London: Penguin UK.
3   Climate Action Tracker. (2022). *2100 warming projections* (Online) Available at: https://tinyurl.com/27n33f6h [Accessed: 15th July 2022]
4   World Commission on Environment and Development. (1987). *Our Common Future*. Oxford and New York: Oxford University Press.

A Natural Ally in the Climate Fight

1   The Nature Conservancy. (2017). *Nature's make or break potential for climate change*. (Online) Available at: https://tinyurl.com/2mfyy5et [Accessed: 15th July 2022]
2   Global Carbon Project. (2021). *Supplemental data of global carbon budget 2021* (Version 1.0 Data set). (Online) Available at: https://tinyurl.com/39c8yhpm [Accessed: 15th July 2022]

3   Stephens, L., Fuller, D., Boivin, N., Rick, T., Gauthier, N., Kay, A., Marwick, B., Armstrong, C. G., Barton, C. M., Denham, T., Douglass, K., Driver, J., Janz, L., Roberts, P., Rogers, J. D., Thakar, H., Altaweel, M., Johnson, A. L., Sampietro Vattuone, M. M., Aldenderfer, M., … Ellis, E. (2019). Archaeological assessment reveals Earth's early transformation through land use. *Science*, *365*(6456), pp.897–902. https://doi.org/10.1126/science.aax1192

4   WWF. (2018). Living planet report – 2018: Aiming higher. Grooten, M., & Almond, R.E.A. (Eds). Gland, Switzerland: WWF.

5   Conservation International. *A critical investment in 'blue carbon'.* (Online) Available at: https://tinyurl.com/yck7bz2b [Accessed: 15th July 2022]

6   CAIT data: Climate Watch. (2020). *GHG Emissions.* Washington, DC: World Resources Institute. (Online) Available at: https://tinyurl.com/yc892kj4 [Accessed: 15th July 2022]

7   United Nations Environment Programme. (2015). The emissions gap report 2015. Nairobi: UNEP.

8   World Bank. *Carbon pricing dashboard.* (Online) Available at: https://tinyurl.com/3byvapra [Accessed: 15th July 2022]

9   California Air Resources Board. (2021). *California's compliance offset program.* Government of California (Online) Available at: https://tinyurl.com/5cfudmh8 [Accessed: 20th November 2022]

10 Conservation International. (2022). *Vida Manglar impact report.* (Online) Available at: https://tinyurl.com/4kf2h8nn [Accessed: 15th July 2022]

11 Chay, F., Cullenward, D., Hamman, J., & Freeman, J. (2021). *Insights from analyzing a new round of carbon removal projects.* CarbonPlan (Online) Available at: https://tinyurl.com/378zzaaa [Accessed: 11th November 2022]

12 Smith, B. (2020). *Microsoft will be carbon neutral by 2030.* Microsoft. (Online) Available at: https://tinyurl.com/5dzcxmex [Accessed: 11th November 2022]

13 Science Based Targets. *Companies taking action.* (Online) Available at: https://tinyurl.com/3u7py9rc [Accessed: 15th July 2022]

14 Microsoft. (2021). *Microsoft carbon removal: Lessons from an early corporate purchase.* (Online) Available at: https://tinyurl.com/442a9vzf [Accessed: 15th July 2022]

A Rough Guide to Ecotourism

1   Weiss, T. (2004). Tourism in America before World War II, *The Journal of Economic History, 64*(2), pp.289–327.

2   Luckham, N. *Overtourism: A centuries-old issue.* Responsible Travel. (Online) Available at: https://tinyurl.com/bdfsxc9y [Accessed: 15th July 2022]

3   Budowski, G. (1976). Tourism and environmental conservation: conflict, coexistence, or symbiosis?, *Environmental Conservation, 3* (1), pp.27–31.

4   IBIS World. (2021). *Global tourism – Market size statistics for global tourism.* (Online) Available at: https://tinyurl.com/3ex6ea7p [Accessed: 15th July 2022]

5   Lock, S. (2021). *Global tourism industry – statistics and facts.* Statista (Online) Available at: https://tinyurl.com/4udcufc4 [Accessed: 15th July 2022]

6   Karantzavelou, V. (2021). *Sustainable travel survey 2021 – 83% say sustainable travel is important.* Travel Daily News. (Online) Available at: https://tinyurl.com/3km8nu9h [Accessed: 15th July 2022]

7   Ecosystem Marketplace. (2021). *Voluntary carbon markets top $1 billion in 2021 with newly reported trades: A special ecosystem marketplace COP26 bulletin.* (Online) Available at: https://tinyurl.com/2p84579k [Accessed: 15th July 2022]

8   IPBES. (2022). *Summary for policymakers of the thematic assessment of the sustainable use of wild species of the Intergovernmental Science-Policy Platform on Biodiversity and Ecosystem Services.* J.-M. Fromentin, M.R. Emery, J. Donaldson, M.-C. Danner, A. Hallosserie, D. Kieling, G. Balachander, F. Barron, R.P. Chaudhary, M. Gasalla, M. Halmy, C. Hicks, M.S. Park, B. Parlee, J. Rice, T. Ticktin, & D. Tittensor (Eds). Bonn, Germany: IPBES secretariat. (Online) Available at: https://doi.org/10.5281/zenodo.6425599 [Accessed: 15th July 2022]

9   World Travel and Tourism Council. (2019). *The economic impact of global wildlife tourism. Travel & tourism as an economic tool for the protection of wildlife.* (Online) Available at: https://tinyurl.com/fv34c9ym [Accessed: 15th July 2022]

10 Brunnschweiler, J.M., & Barnett, A. (2013). Opportunistic visitors: Long-term behavioural response of bull sharks to food provisioning in Fiji. *PLOS ONE, 8*(3), e58522. https://doi.org/10.1371/journal.pone.0058522

11 Friedlander, A.M., Golbuu, Y., Ballesteros, E., Caselle, J.E., Gouezo, M., Olsudong, D., & Sala, E. (2017). Size, age, and habitat determine effectiveness of Palau's Marine Protected Areas. *PLOS ONE*, *12*(3), e0174787. https://doi.org/10.1371/journal.pone.0174787

12 Organization for Economic Co-operation and Development. (OECD). (2019). *Biodiversity: Finance and the economic and business case for action, report prepared for the G7 Environment Ministers' Meeting, 5-6 May 2019.*

13 Fennell, D. (2008). *Ecotourism.* (3rd ed.) New York: Routledge.

14 Buckley, R. (2010). *Conservation tourism.* Wallingford: CAB International.

15 Buckley, R.C., Castley, J.G., Pegas, F.D.V., Mossaz, A.C., & Steven, R. (2012). A population accounting approach to assess tourism contributions to conservation of IUCN-redlisted mammal species, *PLOS ONE*, *7*(9). e44134. https://doi.org/10.1371/journal.pone.0044134

16 Buckley, R. C., Morrison, C., & Castley, J. G. (2016). Net effects of ecotourism on threatened species survival, *PLOS ONE*, *11*(2). e0147988. https://doi.org/10.1371/journal.pone.0147988

17 Bookbinder, M.P., Dinerstein, E., Rijal, A., Cauley, H. and Rajouria, A., 1998. Ecotourism's support of biodiversity conservation. *Conservation biology*, 12(6), pp.1399–1404.

18 Long, G. (2022). Venezuela's environmental crisis: 'The beginning of a wave of destruction'. *Financial Times*. (Online) Available at: https://tinyurl.com/mrybfdsj [Accessed: 15th July 2022]

19 Rogers, P., & van Strien, M. (2022). *Promoting the business of conservation tourism in Southeast Asia.* Mandai Nature. (Online) Available at: https://tinyurl.com/2p8dxs42 [Accessed: 15th July 2022]

20 Mosher, L. (2020). *Blue habits phase 2 wrap-up: Driving behaviour change through nature travel.* Oceanic Society. (Online) Available at: https://tinyurl.com/57s864jh [Accessed: 15th July 2022]

21 Brandon, K. (1996). Ecotourism and conservation: A review of key issues. *Environment Department Papers No. 033.* Washington, DC: World Bank.

22 Vianna, G.M.S., Meekan, M.G., Pannell, D., Marsh, S., & Meeuwig, J.J. (2010). WANTED DEAD OR ALIVE? The relative value of reef sharks as a fishery and an ecotourism asset in Palau. Perth, Australia: Australian Institute of Marine Science.

23 Duffy, R. (2015). Nature-based tourism and neoliberalism: Concealing contradictions. *Tourism Geographies*, 17(4), 529-543. DOI 10.1080/14616688.2015.1053972

Rewild and Regenerate

1 Barkham, P. (2020). First wild stork chicks to hatch in UK in centuries poised to emerge. *The Guardian*. (Online). Available at: https://tinyurl.com/3sku6cr5 [Accessed: 15th July 2022]

2 Beaver Trust. (2020). *A tale of two beavers: At Knepp estate.* (Online) Available at: https://tinyurl.com/3f7tjye4 [Accessed: 15th July 2022]

3 Soil Health Institute. (2021). *Economics of soil health systems in midwest corn and soy.* (Online) Available at: https://tinyurl.com/3s29wcdy [Accessed: 15th July 2022]

4 Montanarella, L., Badraoui, M., Chude, V., Costa, I.D.S.B., Mamo, T., Yemefack, M., Aulang, M.S., Yagi, K., Hong, S.Y., Vijarnsorn, P., & Zhang, G.L. (2015). Status of the world's soil resources: main report. *Embrapa Solos-Livro científico (ALICE).*

5 Sanderman, J., Hengl, T., & Fiske, G. J. (2017). Soil carbon debt of 12,000 years of human land use. *Proceedings of the National Academy of Sciences, 114* (36). pp.9575–9580. DOI 10.1073/pnas.1706103114

6 Ellen Macarthur Foundation. Regenerating an ecosystem to grow organic sugar: The Balbo Group. (Online) Available at: https://tinyurl.com/2ycr92u9 [Accessed: 15th July 2022]

7 Donovan, M. (2020). *What is sustainable intensification?* The International Maize and Wheat Improvement Centre. (Online) Available at: https://tinyurl.com/3cykpcs3 [Accessed: 15th July 2022]

8 Australian Centre for International Agricultural Research. *Achieving sustainable agricultural intensification in eastern and southern Africa: What is needed?* Australian Government (Online) Available at: https://tinyurl.com/yy64udhf [Accessed: 15th July 2022]

9 Burgess, P.J., Harris, J., Graves, A.R., & Deeks, L.K. (2019). Regenerative agriculture: Identifying the impact; enabling the potential. Report for SYSTEMIQ.

10 Food and Agriculture Organisation of the United Nations. (2020). *Global meat production, 1961 to 2018.* (Online) Available at: https://tinyurl.com/28dwmuvs [Accessed: 15th July 2022]

11 Cassidy, E.S., West, P.C., Gerber, J.S., & Foley, J.A. (2013). Redefining agricultural yields: From tonnes to people nourished per hectare. *Environmental Research Letters, 8* (3). p.034015. DOI 10.1088/1748-9326/8/3/034015

12 Marchant, N. (2021). *The world's food waste problem is bigger than we thought – here's what we can do about it.* World Economic Forum. (Online) Available at: https://tinyurl.com/4pvyjs7f [Accessed: 15th July 2022]

13 Sun, Z., Scherer, L., Tukker, A., Spawn-Lee, S.A., Bruckner, M., Gibbs, H.K., & Behrens, P. (2022). Dietary change in high-income nations alone can lead to substantial double climate dividend. *Nature Food*, 3 (1), pp.29–37. DOI 10.1038/s43016-021-00431-5

14 Impossible Burger. (2019). *Impossible Burger Environmental Life Cycle Assessment 2019.* (Online) Available at: https://tinyurl.com/529za8yp [Accessed: 15th July 2022]

15 Tree, I. (2018). *Wilding: The return of nature to a British farm.* London: Picador.

16 McGinnis, M. (2018). *Over half of U.S. farms lose money, USDA study shows.* Agriculture.com. (Online) Available at: https://tinyurl.com/bdd7mmdm [Accessed: 15th July 2022]

17 Sengupta, R. (2020). Every day, 28 people dependent on farming die by suicide in India. *DownToEarth.* (Online) Available at: https://tinyurl.com/2zswxyp2 [Accessed: 15th July 2022]

18 Chenery, S., & Gorman, V. (2020). *How the regenerative farming movement transformed Charles Massy's sheep station.* ABC News. (Online) Available at: https://tinyurl.com/bdc9truh [Accessed: 15th July 2022]

19 Massy, C. (2017). *Call of the reed warbler: A new agriculture – a new Earth.* Brisbane: University of Queensland Press.

20 McMahon, P. (2016). The investment case for ecological farming. Australia: *SLM Partners.*

21 Land O'Lakes, Inc. (2022). *Truterra Carbon Programs Frequently Asked Questions.* (Online) Available at: https://tinyurl.com/y4hb8va2 [Accessed: 15th July 2022]

22 Abram, M. (2021). How a carbon payments scheme will work for 100 UK farmers. *Farmers Weekly.* (Online) Available at: https://tinyurl.com/568t4aha [Accessed: 15th July 2022]

23 Slessarev, E., Zelikova, J., Hamman, J., Cullenward, D., & Freeman, J. (2021). Depth matters for soil carbon accounting. *CarbonPlan.* (Online) Available at: https://tinyurl.com/n8tfcxcy [Accessed: 15th July 2022]

24 Danone. (2021). *Regenerative agriculture: Developing new agricultural models to regenerate the planet.* (Online) Available at: https://tinyurl.com/8kw3p6vm [Accessed: 15th July 2022]

25 Newton, P., Civita, N., Frankel-Goldwater, L., Bartel, K., & Johns, C. (2020). What is regenerative agriculture? A review of scholar and practitioner definitions based on processes and outcomes. *Frontiers in Sustainable Food Systems*, 4. p.194. DOI 10.3389/fsufs.2020.577723

26 Harvey, F. (2019). Can we ditch intensive farming – and still feed the world? *The Guardian*. (Online) Available at: https://tinyurl.com/kfv89cns [Accessed: 15th July 2022]

27 Department for Environment, Food and Rural Affairs (DEFRA). Get ready for our 3 new environment management schemes. UK Government website (online). Available at: https://tinyurl.com/bdchfw43 [Accessed 31st January 2023]

Urban Jungles

1 Ministry of the Environment and Water Resources, Ministry of National Development. (2016). *Singapore's climate action plan: A climate-resilient Singapore, for a sustainable future*. Government of Singapore. (Online) Available at: https://tinyurl.com/3yz9aema [Accessed: 15th July 2022]

2 Joson, J. (2022). *How Singapore is pioneering the way to creating a greener urban environment*. Arch Daily. (Online) Available at: https://tinyurl.com/52xszwtr [Accessed: 15th July 2022]

3 Seng, L. T. (2012). From botanic gardens to gardens by the Bay: Singapore's experience in becoming a garden city. *BiblioAsia, 8(2)*. (Online) Available at: https://tinyurl.com/2xxkfuc9 [Accessed: 15th July 2022]

4 United States Environmental Protection Agency. *Different Shades of Green. Green Infrastructure Research at the Environment Protection Agency* [Brochure]. (Online) Available at: https://tinyurl.com/2cpp62xc [Accessed: 15th July 2022]

5 European Environment Agency. (2021). *What is green infrastructure?* (Online) Available at: https://tinyurl.com/2daarv6z [Accessed: 15th July 2022]

6 Lim, M., & Xenarios, S. (2021). Economic assessment of urban space and blue–green infrastructure in Singapore. *Journal of Urban Ecology*, 7(1). DOI 10.1093/jue/juab020

7 Dreiseitl, H., Leonardsen, J.A., & Wanschura, B. (2015). Cost-benefit analysis of Bishan-AMK Park.

8   Bass, B., Krayenhoff, E. S., Martilli, A., Stull, R. B., & Auld, H. (2003). The impact of green roofs on Toronto's urban heat island. In *Proceedings of the first North American green roof infrastructure conference, awards and trade show: greening rooftops for sustainable communities.* Canada.

9   Ramboll Group, C40 Cities. (2020). Heat resilient cities: Measuring benefits of urban heat adaptation. Case study: Medellín green corridors.

10 Killicoat, P., Puzio, E., & Stringer, R. (2002). The economic value of trees in urban areas: Estimating the benefits of Adelaide's street trees. In *Proceedings Treenet Symposium: Vol. 94,* (p.106).

11 McDonald, R., Kroeger, T., Boucher, T., Wang, L., & Salem, R. (2016). Planting healthy air: A global analysis of the role of urban trees in addressing particulate matter pollution and extreme heat. *The Nature Conservancy.* (Online) Available at: https://tinyurl.com/yv2rwb5w [Accessed: 15th July 2022]

12 Vivid Economics. (2017). Natural capital accounts for public green space in London. *Report prepared for Greater London Authority, National Trust and Heritage Lottery Fund.* (Online) Available at: https://tinyurl.com/2p8nkj5a [Accessed: 15th July 2022]

13 Are you being served? (2005). *The Economist* (Online) Available at: https://tinyurl.com/36cyjj5v [Accessed: 15th July 2022]

14 Appleton, A.F. (2002). How New York City used an ecosystem services strategy carried out through an urban–rural partnership to preserve the pristine quality of its drinking water and save billions of dollars and what lessons it teaches about using ecosystem services. In *The Katoomba Conference.* New York City.

15 Temmerman, S., Meire, P., Bouma, T.J., Herman, P.M., Ysebaert, T., & De Vriend, H.J. (2013). Ecosystem-based coastal defence in the face of global change. *Nature, 504*(7478), pp.79–83. DOI 10.1038/nature12859

16 Menéndez, P., Losada, I.J., Torres-Ortega, S., Narayan, S., & Beck, M.W. (2020). The global flood protection benefits of mangroves. *Scientific reports, 10*(1), pp.1–11. DOI 10.1038/s41598-020-61136-6

17 Global Commission on Adaptation. (2019). Adapt now: A global call for leadership on climate resilience. Washington, DC: World Resources Institute. (Online) Available at: https://tinyurl.com/34yeyucx [Accessed: 15th July 2022]

18   Earth Security. (2021). *The investment value of nature: The case of Zephyr Power Limited*. (Online) Available at: https://tinyurl.com/bdw483rv [Accessed: 30th Aug 2022]

19   Perur, S. (2016). Story of cities #11: the reclamation of Mumbai – from the sea, and its people? *The Guardian*. (Online) Available at: https://tinyurl.com/mtnakf24 [Accessed: 15th July 2022]

20   Fernandes, S., & Chatterjee, B. (2017). World environment day: Mumbai lost 60% of its green cover in 40 years. *Hindustan Times*. (Online) Available at: https://tinyurl.com/bddu6azf [Accessed: 15th July 2022]

21   Rawoot, S., Wescoat Jr., J. L., Noiva, K., & Marks, A. (2015). *Mumbai Case Study. Product of research on 'Enhancing Blue–Green Environmental and Social Performance in High Density Urban Environments'*. Ramboll Group. (Online) Available at: https://tinyurl.com/vrucffrs [Accessed: 15th July 2022]

22   Mumbai Climate Action Plan. (2022). *Climate action plan: Towards a climate resilient Mumbai. Summary for policymakers*. (Online) Available at: https://tinyurl.com/4mjwatj5 [Accessed: 15th July 2022]

23   C40 Cities. (2021). *31 mayors introduce even more trees, parks and green space in cities to save lives and tackle the climate crisis* [Press release]. (Online) Available at: https://tinyurl.com/2p9fc63t [Accessed: 15th July 2022]

24   Channel 4 (2021) 'Freetown to Treetown' – mayor outlines plan to plant a million trees. (Online) Available at: https://tinyurl.com/em3mxxfv [Accessed 27th November 2022]

25   Ertan, S., & Çelik, R.N. (2021). The assessment of urbanization effect and sustainable drainage solutions on flood hazard by GIS. *Sustainability*, *13*(4), p.2293. DOI 10.3390/su13042293

26   University of New Hampshire. *Overcoming barriers to green infrastructure* [Fact sheet]. Green Infrastructure for New Hampshire Coastal Communities. (Online) Available at: https://tinyurl.com/mpa75s65 [Accessed: 15th July 2022]

27   Kabisch, N., Frantzeskaki, N., Pauleit, S., Naumann, S., Davis, M., Artmann, M., Haase, D., Knapp, S., Korn, H., Stadler, J., & Zaunberger, K. (2016). Nature-based solutions to climate change mitigation and adaptation in urban areas: Perspectives on indicators, knowledge gaps, barriers, and opportunities for action. *Ecology and Society*, *21*(2). DOI 10.5751/ES-08373-210239

28 Seddon, N., Chausson, A., Berry, P., Girardin, C.A., Smith, A., & Turner, B. (2020). Understanding the value and limits of nature-based solutions to climate change and other global challenges. *Philosophical Transactions of the Royal Society B*, *375*(1794), p.20190120. DOI 10.1098/rstb.2019.0120

29 Mačiulytė, E., & Durieux, E. (2020). Public procurement of nature-based solutions: Addressing barriers to the procurement of urban NBS: case studies and recommendations. *Directorate-General for Research and Innovation (European Commission)*. (Online) Available at: https://tinyurl.com/yttx7zyf [Accessed: 15th July 2022]

30 Nature for Water Facility. (2022). *The Nature for Water Facility: Local solutions, global impact*. (Online) Available at: https://tinyurl.com/33tsh-tu6 [Accessed: 15th July 2022]

31 European Commission (2020) *Public Procurement of Nature-based Solutions. Addressing barriers to the procurement of urban NBS: case studies and recommendations* (Online) Available at: https://tinyurl.com/c9ahythh [Accessed: 27th November 2022]

32 Poon, L. (2021). *The U.S. Neighborhoods With the Greatest Tree Inequity, Mapped* Bloomberg (Online) Available at: https://tinyurl.com/2casfux2 [Accessed: 27th November 2022]

33 De Zylva, P., Gordon-Smith, C., & Childs, M. (2020). *England's green space gap*. Friends of the Earth (Online) Available at: https://tinyurl.com/yb5zmzz8 [Accessed: 27th November 2022]

Natural Capital: A Framework

1 Bose, S., Dong, G., & Simpson, A. (2019). *The financial ecosystem: The role of finance in achieving sustainability*. (pp.19–46). Cham, Switzerland: Palgrave Macmillan.

2 Natural Capital Forum. *What is natural capital?* (Online) Available at: https://tinyurl.com/m7ysbsbk [Accessed: 15th July2022]

3 Natural Capital Committee. (2019). *Natural capital terminology*. (Online) Available at: https://tinyurl.com/yemhcnn4 [Accessed: 15th July 2022]

4 IPBES. (2019). Global assessment report on biodiversity and ecosystem services of the Intergovernmental Science-Policy Platform on Biodiversity and Ecosystem Services (Version 1). E. S. Brondizio, J. Settele, S. Díaz, & H. T. Ngo (Eds). IPBES Secretariat, Bonn, Germany. (Online)

Available at: https://doi.org/10.5281/zenodo.6417333 [Accessed: 15th July 2022]

5   IPBES. (2022). *Summary for policymakers of the thematic assessment of the sustainable use of wild species of the Intergovernmental Science-Policy Platform on Biodiversity and Ecosystem Services.* J.-M. Fromentin, M.R. Emery, J. Donaldson, M.-C. Danner, A. Hallosserie, D. Kieling, G. Balachander, E. Barron, R.P. Chaudhary, M. Gasalla, M. Halmy, C. Hicks, M.S. Park, B. Parlee, J. Rice, T. Ticktin, &. D. Tittensor (eds). IPBES secretariat, Bonn, Germany. (Online) Available at: https://doi.org/10.5281/zenodo.6425599 [Accessed: 15th July 2022]

6   United States Forest Service. *Medicinal Botany.* United States Department for Agriculture. (Online) Available at: https://tinyurl.com/5xedkc2t [Accessed: 15th July 2022]

7   Bishop, J., Brink, P.T., Gundimeda, H., Kumar, P., Nesshöver, C., Schröter-Schlaack, C., Simmons, B., Sukhdev, P. & Wittmer, H. (2010). The economics of ecosystems and biodiversity: Mainstreaming the economics of nature: A synthesis of the approach, conclusions and recommendations of TEEB. (No. 333.95 E19). Geneva, Switzerland: UNEP.

8   National Science Foundation. (2021). *Economic value of insect pollination services in US much higher than thought, study finds.* (Online) Available at: https://tinyurl.com/y7m46es8 [Accessed: 15th July 2022]

9   Taskforce on Nature Markets. (2022). Nature in an era of crises. (Online) Available at: https://tinyurl.com/mrycpd9b [Accessed: 28th September 2022]

10 Taskforce on Nature Markets. (2022). Nature in an era of crises. (Online) Available at: https://tinyurl.com/mrycpd9b [Accessed: 28th September 2022]

11 Costanza, R., d'Arge, R., De Groot, R., Farber, S., Grasso, M., Hannon, B., Limburg, K., Naeem, S., O'neill, R.V., Paruelo, J., & Raskin, R.G. (1997). The value of the world's ecosystem services and natural capital. *Nature*, *387*(6630), pp.253–260.

12 International Monetary Fund. (2021). World Economic Outlook Database. *World Economic and Financial Surveys.*

13 Phillips, J. (2017). Principles of natural capital accounting. *Office for National Statistics.*

14 Dasgupta, P. (2021). The economics of biodiversity: The Dasgupta review. London: HM Treasury.

15 The White House. (2022). *A new national strategy to reflect natural assets on America's balance sheet.* (Online) Available at: https://tinyurl.com/j6rdz7zt [Accessed: 27th November 2022]

16 Claes, J., Eren, I., Hopman, E., Katz, J., & Van Aken, T. (2022). *Where the world's largest companies stand on nature.* McKinsey Sustainability. Available at: https://tinyurl.com/ykx5xuy9 [Accessed: 28th September 2022]

17 Taskforce on Nature-related Financial Disclosures. *About.* (Online) Available at: https://tinyurl.com/5y2adp3f [Accessed: 15th July 2022]

18 Spurgeon, J., Clarke, P., & Hime, S. (2021). *Principles of integrated capitals assessments.* Capitals Coalition (Online) Available at: https://tinyurl.com/2jcsaaw2 [Accessed: 15th July 2022]

19 Bayon, R., Carroll, N., & Fox, J. (2012). Conservation and biodiversity banking: A guide to setting up and running biodiversity credit trading systems. Earthscan.

20 CIEEM. *Biodiversity net gain – principles and guidance for UK construction and developments.* (Online) Available at: https://tinyurl.com/dsx2xu7r [Accessed: 15th July 2022]

21 Paulson Institute. Financing Nature: Closing the Global Biodiversity Financing Gap. (Online) Available at: https://tinyurl.com/urfz272s [Accessed: 15th July 2022]

22 Ducros, A. and Steele, P. (2022) Biocredits to finance nature and people. International Institute for Environment and Development and United Nation Development Programme (Online) Available at: https://tinyurl.com/2p8z793j [Accessed 7th December 2022]

23 Operation Wallacea. *Biodiversity credits.* (Online) Available at: https://tinyurl.com/5ymjukrm [Accessed: 15th July 2022]

24 Monbiot, G. (2014). *The pricing of everything.* Monbiot.com (Online) Available at: https://tinyurl.com/9d39nu5n [Accessed: 15th July 2022]

25 Monbiot, G. (2018). The UK government wants to put a price on nature – but that will destroy it. *The Guardian.* (Online) Available at: https://tinyurl.com/3sdu6cdj [Accessed: 15th July 2022]

26 Büscher, B. and Fletcher, R. (2016). *Nature is priceless, which is why turning it into 'natural capital' is wrong.* The Conversation. (Online) Available at: https://tinyurl.com/3b8unh3h [Accessed: 15th July 2022]

27 Lewsey, F. *Dasgupta Review: Nature's value must be at the heart of economics.* University of Cambridge. (Online) Available at: https://tinyurl.com/3x3tkakf [Accessed: 11th November 2022]

Tech x Nature

1   The Harvard Animal Landscape Observatory. *Harvard University Davies Lab technology.* (Online) Available at: https://tinyurl.com/2p-8jvzcc [Accessed: 15th July 2022]

2   Pennisi, E. (2021). Getting the big picture of biodiversity. *Science, 374*(6750), pp.926–931. DOI 10.1126/science.acx9637

3   World Resources Institute, Google. Dynamic World V1. (2022). *Earth engine data catalog.* (Online) Available at: https://tinyurl.com/c8hmye3c [Accessed: 15th July 2022]

4   Global Forest Watch. *About.* (Online) Available at: https://tinyurl.com/f8knvjmd [Accessed: 15th July 2022]

5   Conservation X Labs. *The Sentinel.* (Online) Available at: https://tinyurl.com/bdhfm9ws [Accessed: 15th July 2022]

6   Lynggaard, C., Bertelsen, M.F., Jensen, C.V., Johnson, M.S., Frøslev, T.G., Olsen, M.T., & Bohmann, K. (2022). Airborne environmental DNA for terrestrial vertebrate community monitoring. *Current Biology, 32*(3), pp.701–707. DOI 10.1016/j.cub.2021.12.014

7   Wetterstrand, K. A. *DNA sequencing costs: Data from the NHGRI genome sequencing program.* National Human Genome Research Institute. (Online) Available at: https://tinyurl.com/4nmm5w34 [Accessed: 15th July 2022]

8   Metinko, C. (2022). Funding starts to cascade into Web3 startups. *Crunchbase News.* (Online) Available at: https://tinyurl.com/2p8e6r8n [Accessed: 15th July 2022]

9   Zou, K., & Purdom. S. (2022). IPCC 6: Running out of time #97. *Climate Tech VC.*

10 Badgley, G., & Cullenward, D. (2022). *Zombies on the blockchain.* CarbonPlan (Online) Available at: https://tinyurl.com/mv8wdb39 [Accessed: 15th November 2022]

11 Rockefeller Philanthropy Advisors and Campden Wealth. (2020). *Global trends and strategic time horizons in family philanthropy 2020.* (Online) Available at: https://tinyurl.com/mucd3emm [Accessed: 15th July 2022]

12 Moss. Moss's Amazon NFT. (Online) Available at: https://tinyurl.com/yktw8yps [Accessed: 15th July 2022]

Fighting Fire with Finance

1   United States Forest Service. (2015). *The rising cost of wildfire operations: Effects on the Forest Service's non-fire work.* United States Department of Agriculture. (Online) Available at: https://tinyurl.com/3vn94rrh [Accessed: 15th July 2022]

2   United States Department of Agriculture. (2017). *Forest service wildland fire suppression costs exceed $2 billion* [Press release]. (Online) Available at: https://tinyurl.com/2p9h3dum [Accessed: 15th July 2022]

3   Deutz, A., Heal, G. M., Niu, R., Swanson, E., Townshend, T., Zhu, L., Delmar, A., Meghji, A., Sethi, S. A., & Tobin-de la Puente, J. (2020). Financing nature: Closing the global biodiversity financing gap. *The Paulson Institute, The Nature Conservancy, and the Cornell Atkinson Center for Sustainability.*

4   Martin, B. (2018). *Insuring coral reefs in Mexico.* Green Economy Coalition. (Online) Available at: https://tinyurl.com/2hsxck2h [Accessed: 15th July 2022]

5   Smith, M. (2021). How insurance is protecting the mesoamerican reef. *Scuba Diving.* (Online) Available at: https://tinyurl.com/2s4drcfm [Accessed: 15th July 2022]

6   Berg, C., Bertolotti, L., Bieri, T., Bowman, J., Braun, R., Cardillo, J., Chaudhury, M., Falinski, K., Geselbracht, L., Hum, K., Lustic, C., Roberts, E., Young, S., & Way, M. (2020). *Insurance for natural infrastructure: Assessing the feasibility of insuring coral reefs in Florida and Hawai'i.* Arlington, VA: The Nature Conservancy.

7   World Bank. (2022). *Insuring nature's survival: The role of insurance in meeting the financial need to preserve biodiversity.* Washington, DC: World Bank.

8   World Bank. (2022). *Wildlife conservation bond boosts South Africa's efforts to protect black rhinos and support local communities* [Press release]. (Online) Available at: https://tinyurl.com/3sa6vjn5 [Accessed: 15th July 2022]

9   Bala, A. R., Behsudi, A., & Owen, N. (2022). Meeting the future. *Finance & Development, 59*(001).

10   Ministerio de Hacienda. (2022). *Chile makes a historic issue for US$ 2,000 million and becomes the first country to issue a bond linked to sustainability.* Government of Chile. (Online) Available at: https://tinyurl.com/2n76ac3s [Accessed: 15th July 2022]

11 Beattie, A. (2021). What Was the First Company to Issue Stock? *Investopedia*. (Online) Available at: https://tinyurl.com/3cedsm8y [Accessed: 15th July 2022]

The Indigenous Case for Nature

1   Rundle, H. (2019). Indigenous knowledge can help solve the biodiversity crisis. *Scientific American*. (Online) Available at: https://tinyurl.com/3sapejmz [Accessed: 15th July 2022]

2   Jones, B. (2021). *Indigenous people are the world's biggest conservationists, but they rarely get credit for it.* Vox. (Online) Available at: https://tinyurl.com/4aumhy49 [Accessed: 15th July 2022]

3   Morrison, S., & Morrison, S. (2021). Why referring to New Zealand as Aotearoa is a meaningful step for travelers. *Condé Nast Traveler.* (Online) Available at: https://tinyurl.com/bdej5236 [Accessed: 15th July 2022]

4   Fyers, A. (2018). The amount allocated to Treaty of Waitangi settlements is tiny, compared with other Government spending. *Stuff.* (Online) Available at: https://tinyurl.com/mr3z4c8f [Accessed: 15th July 2022]

5   Galbreath, R., & Brown, D. (2004). The tale of the lighthouse-keeper's cat: Discovery and extinction of the Stephens Island wren (Traversia lyalli). *Notornis*, *51*(4), pp.193–200.

6   Low, A., & Taylor, L. (2017). Waikawa Bay marina extension – Kaimoana management plan. *Mitchell Daysh Limited.*

7   Taiepa, T., Lyver, P., Horsley, P., Davis, J., Brag, M., & Moller, H. (1997). Co-management of New Zealand's conservation estate by Māori and Pakeha: A review. *Environmental conservation*, *24*(3), pp.236–250. DOI 10.1017/S0376892997000325

8   Taiepa, T., Lyver, P., Horsley, P., Davis, J., Brag, M., & Moller, H. (1997). Co-management of New Zealand's conservation estate by Māori and Pakeha: A review. Environmental conservation, 24(3), pp.236–250.

9   New Zealand Department of Conservation. (1996). Tiritiri Matangi island. In *Ecosystem restoration on mainland New Zealand.* Government of New Zealand (Online) Available at: https://tinyurl.com/2ejfy87a [Accessed: 15th July 2022]

10 Fisher, D. (2022). 'We do not want to stand by': Prime Minister Jacinda Ardern's Waitangi speech and Covid response for Māori. *New Zealand Herald*. (Online) Available at: https://tinyurl.com/3c3jypmf [Accessed: 15th July 2022]

11 Gammage, B. (2011). *The biggest estate on Earth: How Aborigines made Australia*. Crow's Nest, NSW: Allen and Unwin.

12 Mallapaty, S. (2021). Australian bush fires belched out immense quantity of carbon. *Nature*, 597(7877), pp.459–460.

13 Vernick, D. (2020). *3 billion animals harmed by Australia's fires*. WWF. (Online) Available at: https://tinyurl.com/2p92rw55 [Accessed: 15th July 2022]

14 Shapiro, H. (2019). Ending Adivasi eviction: Protecting the forest by protecting land rights. *The Cornell Diplomat*. (Online) Available at: https://tinyurl.com/4jp24k3d [Accessed: 15th July 2022]

15 Godio, M. J., Chepkorir, M., Kitelo, P., & Kimaiyo, E. (2020). *Kenya case study: Forced evictions in the middle of COVID-19 pandemic leaves Sengwer community with no homes*. Forest Peoples Programme. (Online) Available at: https://tinyurl.com/y9kd65w7 [Accessed:15th July 2022]

16 McQue, K. (2022). Tanzania's Maasai appeal to west to stop eviction for conservation plans. *The Guardian*. (Online) Available at: https://tinyurl.com/a2h6hxxj [Accessed: 15th July 2022]

17 The Uluru Statement. (2017). *The Uluru statement from the heart*. (Online) Available at: https://tinyurl.com/me8djrkj [Accessed: 15th July 2022]

18 United Nations Environment Programme. (2017). *Indigenous people and nature: A tradition of conservation*. (Online) Available at: https://tinyurl.com/588enj5r [Accessed: 15th July 2022]

19 Veit, P., & Ding, H. (2016). *Protecting indigenous land rights makes good economic sense*. World Resources Institute. (Online) Available at: https://tinyurl.com/4rvr27xy [Accessed: 15th July 2022]

20 Alves-Pinto, H.N., Cordeiro, C.L., Geldmann, J., Jonas, H.D., Gaiarsa, M.P., Balmford, A., Watson, J.E., Latawiec, A.E., & Strassburg, B. (2022). The role of different governance regimes in reducing native vegetation conversion and promoting regrowth in the Brazilian Amazon. *Biological Conservation*, 267, p.109473. DOI 10.1016/j.biocon.2022.109473

21 Baragwanath, K., & Bayi, E. (2020). Collective property rights reduce deforestation in the Brazilian Amazon. *Proceedings of the National Academy of Sciences*, 117(34), p.20495. DOI 10.1073/pnas.191787411

22 Nia Tero. *Stories of action and ingenuity from around the globe.* (Online) Available at: https://tinyurl.com/4rpna62c [Accessed: 15th July 2022]

23 Schroeder, D., Chennells, R., Louw, C., Snyders, L., & Hodges, T. (2020). The Rooibos benefit sharing agreement – Breaking new ground with respect, honesty, fairness, and care. *Cambridge Quarterly of Healthcare Ethics*, *29*(2), pp.285–301. DOI 10.1017/S0963180119001075

24 Roy, E. A. (2017). New Zealand river granted same legal rights as human being. *The Guardian.* (Online) Available at: https://tinyurl.com/yx5x3xn6 [Accessed: 15th July 2022]

25 Surma, K. (2021). *Ecuador's high court affirms constitutional protections for the rights of nature in a landmark decision.* Inside Climate News. (Online) Available at: https://tinyurl.com/yckjwss2 [Accessed: 15th July 2022]

26 Safi, M. (2017). Ganges and Yamuna rivers granted same legal rights as human beings. *The Guardian.* (Online) Available at: https://tinyurl.com/335mp5zj [Accessed: 15th July 2022]

27 *India's Ganges and Yamuna rivers are 'not living entities'.* (2017.) BBC News. (Online) Available at: https://tinyurl.com/ycx934d7 [Accessed: 15th July 2022]

28 Nelson, R. (2020). *Make prayers to the raven: A Koyukon view of the Northern Forest.* Chicago, IL: University of Chicago Press.

Synthesis

1 Goodall, J. (2004). *Reason for hope: An extraordinary life.* Hachette.